New Reformation

New Reformation

*Notes of
a Neolithic Conservative*

Paul Goodman

Vintage Books
A Division of Random House / New York

ISBN: 0-394-71121-1

Library of Congress Catalog Card Number: 70-102299

Manufactured in the United States of America

First Vintage Books Edition, August 1971

For Marc Raskin,
who makes a good try at being an old-fashioned citizen

Contents

Preface

PART ONE: Sciences and Professions

PART TWO: Education of the Young

PART THREE: Legitimacy

Notes of a Neolithic Conservative

Preface

It makes sense to say that the conditions of modern society are "dehumanizing," and I have harped on the notion in many books of social criticism (this is the tenth). Yet, as I walk the streets of the city, it does not seem to me that the people are less human, less people, than when I was an adolescent nearly fifty years ago. Certainly New York has changed mightily, but the New Yorkers appear—it is hard to remember back—only sadder, more harassed, more anxious. They do not look the least bit more robotized, nor do they have glazed eyes. The ones who have glazed eyes are high on heroin, not on regimentation, brainwashing, or the standard of living.

There are no people who are not socialized; yet there is a difference between just people and people playing their social roles. Classical social science dealt with this problem seriously: it is implicit in the concepts of exploitation, alienation, and anomie, and resentment, rebellion, and liberty. It was the staple of classical tragedy, and realist and naturalist novelists were fascinated by the story of people in conflict with their status and social function. Anarchist and Jeffersonian politics have relied on the tension between human nature and institutional roles as the possibility for social change. But my contemporary sociologists, anthropologists, liberal politicians, and even educators do not seem to recognize that there is a puzzle. Many novelists seem to be "making the scene" rather than presenting characters who cope with it and try to live their lives. Obviously I do not understand them.

What strikes me, for instance, is how after ten years in a maximum-security prison, as soon as there was a tiny possibility of escape, the spirit and prose style of Alexander Berkman sprang alive as if he had not been dehumanized at all. After twenty-one years of totalitarian indoctrination, the youth of Czechoslovakia, who had never known any other dispensation, came on as they did in 1968. The Americans, in spite of every apparent influence, have not tended toward a Brave New World, but instead there is a sudden revival of populism. The evidence seems to be that actual fright can lastingly alter behavior, but mere institutional threats, conditioning, and brainwashing are ineffectual.

Social and technological conditions do determine behavior in every detail; the way they lay out the streets is the way we must walk. I suppose we mean by "dehumanizing" those conditions that are so stressful that people get sick or die; but this is not the same as playing social roles. At present there is widespread discussion of more efficient means of socialization, by use of drugs, electrodes, and genetic alteration. I don't know any evidence that these means would be biologically feasible, that they can indeed produce live products that will perform social roles. But even if this were possible, I think that we would rather easily judge at what point we are no longer dealing with people but with humanoids; and sociologists, anthropologists, and novelists would lose interest, except in the experimenters themselves. There might be a set of new sciences, but no politics or literature.

Social science deals with the tension between people and personnel, between human powers and human institutions. In my opinion, it is always practical and political—in a good society where the institutions actualize and enhance human powers, there would be little social science. (My anarchist bias is that, by and large, this happens best when persons and their functioning communities are just let be.)

When institutions drastically fail to provide, and do severe damage, as by brutal exploitation, unsuccessful war, or incompetent tyranny, people respond with political turmoil, and aim at a revolution in government. When conditions are—or are also—"dehumanizing," there is alienation, anomie, mental disease, delinquency, and generation gap; and we come to the cultural and religious crisis that is the subject of this book. My subject is the breakdown of belief, and the emergence of new belief, in sciences and professions, education, and civil legitimacy.

i i

I have mixed feelings about the title *New Reformation* and the overall analogy I draw to the Protestant Reformation. For purposes of exposition, I could dispense with the analogy entirely, with no loss. It is bound to cause misunderstanding. But I have kept it for reasons of my personal poetry.

In moments of indignation and dissent—in writing *Growing Up Absurd* and *Jeremy Owen,* during the Free Speech Movement and the draft Resistance, tax-refusal, and campaigning against the school establishment—I have in fact been inspirited by Wiclif and Hus, I have been sickened by the Whore of Babylon, and the haunting high horn in Mendelssohn's symphony saying *"Ein feste Burg"* has sounded to me like "the faint dawn bugle when the things fall of their weight." In more sober moments, to be sure, I remember that Luther's and Cromwell's bullies were real bastards.

By "Reformation" I mean simply an upheaval of belief that is of religious depth, but that does *not* involve destroying the common faith, but to purge and reform it. (Of course, such a religious reform may be politically revolutionary.) It is evident that, at present, we are not going to give up the mass faith in scientific technology that is the religion of modern times; and yet we cannot continue with it, as it has been perverted. So I look for a "New Reformation." As a corollary, I think that important agents of change will be found among professionals and academics dissenting from the establishment; and this is like the Protestant Reformation. And the worldwide youth movement, perhaps especially in its fanaticism and self-righteous violence, has come to look more like the Reformation than like other historic movements to which it can be compared, the goliards or Sturm und Drang or the narodniks. As Vann Woodward has put it, they are Roundheads with Cavalier hairdos.

The trouble with the analogy to the Protestant Reformation, however, is that one of the chief sources of corruption in our modern system of belief has been precisely the dehumanizing tendencies set in motion by the Protestant Reformation itself. These are the rationalizing, abstract universalizing, grading, and isolating of individuals, Phariseeism, and economism that in modern times have infected the organization of sciences, work, and society, destroying community, traditional culture, animality, and real wealth. Thus, one thing that must be purged in our present Whore of Babylon is the triumph of the Protestant Reformation.

Another difficulty with the analogy of the Protestant Reformation, let me say, is that, although I see lots of troops, I don't see any Wiclif, Hus, or Luther to lead them. But being myself an Erasmian skeptic, I probably wouldn't recognize them anyway.

i i i

Compared with the tempered enthusiasm of my previous books, this one is rather sour on the American young. In 1958 I called them my "crazy young allies" and now I'm saying that, when the chips are down, they're just like their fathers. The change must partly be because I myself am old and tired. The question is why I hector them rather than keeping a decent silence, for they are better than their detractors.

The answer is simple. Now for a decade youth politics and religion have been the only ball game in town. This is changing; more sober citizens are getting on the field, but it is still thanks to the young. Naturally I want the young to move in the direction of my own politics and I'm disappointed if they don't. To me the big news is the awakening by young professionals in law, medicine, ecology, and education. If only it will spread to engineering and mass communications! I am less sanguine about the activist graduate students and young professors in literature and history, since we do not agree on what the humanities are about; but it is better for the humanities to be about the wrong thing than about nothing.

As one of the half-dozen elder statesmen who have provided propositions and points of view that the young have picked up, I really do not know how to cope with the dilemmas that arise when I dissent from their movement and they show me their hostility in no uncertain terms. Just to condone their idiocy would, it seems to me, be condescending, and I have never done it. But the young at present are so insecure and distrustful that they hotly resent criticism, and they are so alienated that they don't understand it anyway.

Their intolerance is breath-taking. Do Your Thing means do their thing. I have seen cases where they exploit their elders' resources and sponsorship, but then betray our explicit purposes because they are convinced that we are fools or finks. They do not regard this as conning.

What then? Suppose we shrug and turn away. Then they have no access to the resources that we ought to share, to which they have a right claim, and to any wisdom we have to give, such as it is. And if those of us who care for them, and whom they somewhat respect, do not take them seriously, if only to hector them, who will take them seriously? Besides, they *are* the ball game. And sometimes they even do know better.

> So I morose
> go back where they are beating their tom-toms
> and shouting "Shut it down." They do not sound
> like Isaac Newton, more a mob of monkeys,
> but they are Adam the next time around
> and what I hope. I see it doesn't please
> them either that I stand here as I am.
> Let them put up with me as I with them.

December 26, 1969

PART ONE

Sciences
and Professions

Chapter 1

i

On March 4, 1969, there was a "work stoppage" and teach-in initiated by dissenting professors at the Massachusetts Institute of Technology, followed at thirty other major universities and technical schools across the country, against misdirected scientific research and the abuse of scientific technology. In this book I want to consider this event in a broader context than the professors did, as part of a religious crisis. An attack on the American scientific establishment is an attack on the worldwide system of belief. I think we are on the eve of a new Reformation, and no institution or status will go unaffected.

March 4 was, of course, only the latest of a series of protests in the twenty-five years since the Manhattan Project to build the atom bomb, during which time the central funding of research and innovation has grown so enormously and its purposes have become so unpalatable. In 1940 the federal budget for research and development was seventy-three million dollars, in 1967 seventeen billion. As the old man predicted in *The Empire City*, the "duration" has lasted longer than the war. Hitler's war was a watershed of modern times. We are accustomed, as H. R. Trevor-Roper has pointed out, to write Hitler off as an aberration, who was of little political significance. But in fact the military emergency that he and his Japanese allies created confirmed the worst tendencies of the giant states, till now they are probably irreversible by ordinary political means.

After Hiroshima, there was the conscience-stricken movement of the atomic scientists and the founding of their Bulletin. The American Association for the Advancement of Science pledged itself to keep the public informed about the dangerous bearings of new developments. There was the Oppenheimer incident. Ads of the East Coast scientists successfully stopped the bomb shelters, warned about the fallout, and helped produce the test ban. There was a scandal about the bombardment of the Van Allen belt. Scientists and technologists formed a powerful (and misguided) ad hoc group for Johnson in the 1964 election. In some universities, sometimes with bitter struggle, classified contracts have been excluded. There is a Society for Social Responsibility in Science. Rachel Carson's book on the pesticides made a stir, until the Department of Agriculture rescued the manufacturers and plantation-owners. Ralph Nader has been on his rampage. Thanks to spectacular abuses like the smog, strip mining, oil pollution, random use of pesticides, and asphalting of arable land, ecologists and conservationists have been getting a hearing. Protest against the sonic boom has slowed the development of the supersonic transport. At present (1969), there is a concerted outcry against the anti-ballistic missiles.

The target of protest has become broader and the grounds of complaint deeper. The target is now not merely the military but the universities, the commercial corporations, and the government. It is said that money is being given by the wrong sponsors to the wrong people for the wrong purposes. In some of the great schools such funding is the main support; for instance at M.I.T. 90 percent of the research budget is from the government, and 65 percent of that is military.

Inevitably, such funding channels the brainpower of most of the brightest science students, who go where the action is, and this predetermines the course of American science and technology for the foreseeable future. At present nearly 200,000 American engineers and scientists spend all their time making weapons. This is a comment on, perhaps an explanation for, the usual statement that more scientists are now alive than since Adam and Eve. And the style of our research and development is not good. It is dominated by production of hardware, logistics, and devising of salable novelties. Often there is secrecy, always nationalism. Since the grants go overwhelmingly through a very few corporations and universities, they favor a limited number of scientific attitudes and preconceptions, with incestuous staffing. There is a premium on "positive results"; surprising "failures" cannot be pursued, so that science ceases to be a wandering dialogue with the unknown.

The policy is economically wasteful. A vast amount of brains and money is spent on crash programs to solve often essentially petty problems, and the claim that there is a spin-off of useful discoveries is laughable, considering the sums involved. The claim that research is neutral, and it doesn't matter what one works on, is shabby, considering the heavy funding in certain directions. Social priorities are scandalous: money is spent on overkill, the supersonic plane, brand-name identical drugs, annual model changes of cars, new detergents, and color television—many have objected to the Moon shot—whereas water, air, cities, food, health, and foreign aid are neglected. And much research is so morally repugnant (consider the work on chemical and biological weapons) that we dare not humanly continue it.

The state of the behavioral sciences is, if anything, worse. Their claim to moral and political neutrality becomes, in effect, a means of diverting attention from glaring social evils, and they are in fact used—or would be if they worked—for warfare and social engineering, manipulation of people for the political and economic purposes of the powers that be. This is an especially sad betrayal since, in the not-too-distant past, the objective social sciences were developed largely to dissolve orthodoxy, irrational authority, and taboo. They were heretical and intellectually revolutionary, as the physical sciences had been in their own heroic age—and they weren't getting government grants.

This was the grim indictment of March 4, 1969. Even so, I do not think the dissenting scientists understand how deep their trouble is. They still take themselves too much for granted. Indeed, a repeated theme of the March 4th complaints was that the science budget was being cut back, especially in basic research. The assumption was that, though the sciences are abused, Science would rightly maintain and increase its expensive preeminence among social institutions. Our society was in a bad way; the abuse of science was part of it; but Science could find the answers.

Underlying the growing dissent, however, there is a historical crisis. There has been a profound change in popular feeling, more than among the professors. Put it this way: Modern societies have been operating as if religion were a minor and moribund part of the scheme of things. But this is unlikely. Men do not do without a system of "meanings" that everybody believes and puts his hope in even if, or especially if, he doesn't know anything about it; what Freud called a "shared psychosis," meaningful because shared, and with the power that resides in dream and longing. And in fact, in advanced countries it is science and technology themselves that have gradually and at last triumphantly become the system of mass faith, not disputed by various political ideologies and nationalisms that have also been mass religions. Marxism called itself "scientific socialism," as against moral and utopian socialisms; and movements of national liberation have especially promised to open the benefits of industrialization and technological progress when once they have gotten rid of the imperialists.

For three hundred years, science and scientific technology had an unblemished and justified reputation as a wonderful adventure, pouring out practical benefits and liberating spirit from the errors of superstition and traditional faith. During the twentieth century, science and scientific technology have been the only generally credited systems of explanation and problem-solving. Yet in our generation they have come to seem to many, and to very many of the best of the young, essentially inhuman, abstract, regimenting, hand in glove with Power, and even diabolical. Young people say that science is anti-life, it is a Calvinist obsession, it has been a weapon of white Europe to subjugate colored races; and manifestly—in view of recent scientific technology—people who think "scientifically" become insane. With science, the other professions are discredited. The academic "disciples" are discredited.

The immediate reasons for this shattering reversal of values are fairly obvious: Hitler's ovens and his other experiments in eugenics, the first atom bombs and their frenzied subsequent developments, the deterioration of the physical environment and the destruction of the biosphere, the catastrophes impending over the cities because of technological failures and psychological stress, the prospect of a brainwashed and drugged 1984. Innovations yield diminishing returns in enhancing life. And instead of rejoicing, there is now widespread conviction that beautiful advances, in genetics, surgery, computers, rocketry, or atomic energy, will surely only increase human woe.

In such a crisis, in my opinion, it will not be sufficient to ban the military from the universities; and it will not even be sufficient, as liberal statesmen and many of the big corporations envisage, to beat the swords into ploughshares and turn to solving problems of transportation, desalinization, urban renewal, garbage disposal, and cleaning up the air and water. If the present difficulty is religious and historical, it is necessary to alter the entire relationship of science, technology, and social needs both in men's minds and in fact. This involves changes in the organization of science, in scientific education, and in the kinds of men who make scientific decisions.

I do not mean that we will turn away from science. In spite of the fantasies of hippies, we are certainly going to continue to live in a technological world. The question is a different one: Is it viable? Can it be made viable?

i i

Whether or not it draws on new scientific research, technology is a branch of moral philosophy, not of science. It aims at prudent goods for the commonweal, to provide efficient means for these goods. At present, however, "scientific technology" occupies a bastard position, in the universities, in funding, and in the public mind. It is half tied to the theoretical sciences and half treated as mere know-how for political and commercial purposes. It has no principles of its own. To remedy this—so Karl Jaspers in Europe and Robert Hutchins in America have urged—technology must have its proper place on the faculty as a learned profession important in modern society, along with medicine, law, the humanities, and natural philosophy, learning from them and having something to teach them. As a moral philosopher, a technician should be able to criticize the programs given him to implement. As a professional in a community of learned professionals, a technologist must have a different kind of training and develop a different character from what we see at present among technicians and engineers. He should know something of the social sciences, law, the fine arts, and medicine, as well as relevant natural sciences.

Prudence is foresight, caution, utility. Thus it is up to the technologists, not merely to regulatory agencies of the government, to provide for safety and to think about remote effects. This is what Ralph Nader sometimes says and Rachel Carson used to ask. An important aspect of caution is flexibility, to avoid the pyramiding catastrophe that occurs when something goes wrong in interlocking technologies, as in urban power failures. Naturally, to take responsibility often requires standing up to the front office, urban politicians, and the Pentagon, and technologists must organize themselves in order to have power to do it.

Often it is pretty clear that a technology has been oversold, like the cars. Then even though the public, seduced by advertising, wants more, technologists must balk, as any professional does when his client wants what isn't good for him. We are now repeating the same self-defeating congestion with the planes and airports: the more the technology is oversold, the less immediate utility it provides, the greater the costs, and the more damaging the remote effects. As this becomes evident, it is time for technologists to confer with sociologists and economists and ask deeper questions. Is so much travel necessary? Are there ways to diminish it? Instead, the recent history of technology has consisted largely of desperate efforts to remedy situations caused by previous overapplications of technology.

Technologists should certainly have a say about simple waste, for even in an affluent society there are priorities—consider the supersonic transport, which has little to recommend it. But the Moon shot has presented the more usual dilemma of authentic conflicting claims. I myself believe that space exploration is a great human adventure, with immense esthetic and moral benefits, whatever the scientific or utilitarian uses. It must be pursued. Yet the context and auspices have been such that perhaps it would be better if it were not pursued. (This is discussed in Chapter 2.)

These days, perhaps the chief moral criterion of a philosophic technology is modesty, having a sense of the whole and not obtruding more than a particular function warrants. Immodesty is always a danger of free enterprise, but when the same disposition to market is financed by big corporations, technologists rush into production with solutions that swamp the environment. This applies to the packaging and garbage, freeways that bulldoze neighborhoods, high rises that destroy landscape, wiping out species for a passing fashion, strip mining, scrapping an expensive machine rather than making a minor repair, draining a watershed for irrigation because (as in southern California) the cultivable land has been covered by asphalt. Given this disposition, it is not surprising that we defoliate a forest in order to expose a guerrilla and spray tear gas from a helicopter on a crowded campus.

Since we are technologically overcommitted, a good general maxim in advanced countries at present is to innovate in order to simplify, but otherwise to innovate as sparingly as possible. Every advanced country is overtechnologized; past a certain point, the quality of life diminishes with new "improvements." Yet no country is rightly technologized, making efficient use of available techniques. There are ingenious devices for unimportant functions, stressful mazes for essential functions, and drastic dislocation when anything goes wrong, which happens with increasing frequency. To add to the complexity, the mass of people tend to become incompetent, and dependent on repairmen. Indeed, unrepairability except by experts has become a desideratum of industrial design.

When I speak of slowing down or cutting back, the issue is not whether research and making working models should be encouraged or not. They should be, in every direction, and given a blank check. The point is to resist the temptation to apply every new device without a second thought. But the big corporate organization of research and development makes prudence and modesty very difficult; it is necessary to get big contracts and rush into production in order to pay the salaries of the big team, and to keep the team from dispersing. Like bureaucracies, technological organizations are finally run to maintain themselves in being, as a team, but they are more dangerous because in capitalist countries they are in a competitive arena and must stir up business.

It used to be the classical socialist objection to capitalism that it curtailed innovation and production in order to make the most out of existing capital. This objection still holds, of course—a serious example is the foot-dragging about producing an electric or steam car which, according to Ford, will take thirty years, though models adequate for urban use are ready for production at present. But by and large, the present menace of free enterprise is proving to be the same as its past glory, its fantastic productivity, its technological explosion. And this is not the classic overproduction that creates a glut on the market; it is overproduction that burdens life and the environment.

I mean the maxim of simplification quite strictly, to simplify the *technical* system. I am unimpressed by the argument that what is technically more complicated is really economically or politically simpler, for example, by complicating the packaging we improve the supermarkets; by throwing away the machine rather than repairing it we give cheaper and faster service all around; or even, by expanding the economy with trivial innovations, we increase employment, allay discontent, save on welfare. Such ideas may be profitable for private companies or political parties, but for society they have created an accelerating rat race. The technical structure of the environment is too important to be a political or economic pawn; the effect on the quality of life is too disastrous. The hidden social costs are not calculated: the auto graveyards, the torn-up streets, the longer miles of commuting, the advertising, the inflation, etc. As I pointed out in *People or Personnel,* a country with a fourth of our per capita income, such as Ireland, is not less well off; in some respects it is much richer, in some respects a little poorer. If possible, it is better to solve political problems by political means. For instance, if teaching machines and audio-visual aids are indeed educative, well and good; but if school boards hope to use them just to save money on teachers, then they are not good at all—nor do they save money.

Of course, the goals of right technology must come to terms with other values of society. I am not a technocrat. But the advantage of raising technology to be a responsible learned profession with its own principles is that it can have a voice in the debate and argue for *its* proper contribution to the community. Consider the important case of modular sizes in building, or prefabrication of a unit bathroom: these conflict with the short-run interests of manufacturers and craft unions, yet to deny them is technically an abomination. The usual recourse is for a government agency to set standards; such agencies accommodate to interests that have a strong voice; and at present technologists have no voice.

The crucial need for technological simplification, however, is not in the advanced countries—which can afford their clutter and probably deserve it—but in underdeveloped countries which must rapidly innovate in order to diminish disease, drudgery, and starvation. They cannot afford to make mistakes. It is now widely conceded that the technological aid we have given to such areas according to our own high style—a style often demanded by the native ruling groups—has done more harm than good. Even when, frequently if not usually, aid has been benevolent, without strings attached—and not military, and not dumping—it has nevertheless disrupted ways of life, fomented tribal wars, accelerated urbanization, decreased the food supply, gone to waste for lack of skills to use it, developed a do-nothing elite.

By contrast, a group of international scientists called

Intermediate Technology argue that what is needed is techniques that use only native labor, resources, traditional customs, and teachable know-how, with the simple aim of remedying drudgery, disease, and hunger, so that people can then develop further in their own style. This avoids cultural imperialism. Such intermediate techniques may be quite primitive, on a level unknown among us for a couple of centuries, and yet they may pose extremely subtle problems, requiring exquisite scientific research and political and human understanding, to devise a very simple technology. Here is a reported case (by E. F. Schumacher, which I trust I remember accurately). In Botswana, a very poor country, pasture was overgrazed, but the economy could be salvaged if the land was fenced. There was no local material for fencing, and imported fencing was prohibitively expensive. The solution was to find a formula and technique to make posts out of mud, and a pedagogic method to teach people how to do it.

In *The Two Cultures,* C. P. Snow berated the humanists for their irrelevance when two-thirds of mankind are starving and what is needed is science and technology. The humanities have perhaps been irrelevant; but unless technology is itself more humanistic and philosophical, it too is of no use. There is only one culture.

And, let me make a remark about amenity as a technical criterion. It is discouraging to see the concern about beautifying a highway and banning billboards, and about the cosmetic appearance of cars, when there is no regard for the ugliness of bumper-to-bumper traffic and the suffering of the drivers. Or the concern for preserving a historical landmark while the neighborhood is torn up and the city has no shape. Without moral philosophy, people have nothing but sentiments.

iii

The complement to prudent technology is the ecological approach in science. To simplify the technical system and modestly pinpoint our artificial intervention in the environment is to make it possible for the environment to survive in its complexity, evolved for a billion years, whereas the overwhelming instant intervention of tightly inter-locked and bulldozing technology has already disrupted many of the delicate sequences and balances. The calculable consequences are already frightening, but of course we don't know enough, and won't in the foreseeable future, to predict the remote effects of much of what we have done.

Cyberneticists come to the same cautious thinking. The use of computers has enabled us to carry out crashingly inept programs on the basis of willful analyses; but we have also become increasingly alert to the fact that things respond, systematically, continually, cumulatively; they can-not simply be manipulated or pushed around. Whether bac-teria, weeds, bugs, the technologically unemployed, or unpleasant thoughts, we cannot simply eliminate and forget them; repressed, they return in new forms. A complicated system works most efficiently if its parts readjust themselves decentrally, with a minimum of central intervention or control, except in cases of breakdown. Usually there is an advantage in a central clearing house of information about the gross total situation, but technical decision and execu-tion require more minute local information. The fantas-tically rehearsed Moon landing hung on a last-second cor-rection on the spot. To make decisions in headquarters means to rely on information from the field that is cumula-tively abstract and may be irrelevant, and to execute by chain-of-command is to use standards that cumulatively do not fit the abilities of real individuals in concrete situations. By and large it is better, given a sense of the whole picture, for those in the field to decide what to do and to do it (com-pare *People or Personnel,* Chapter 3). But with organisms too, this has long been the bias of psychosomatic medicine, the Wisdom of the Body, as Cannon called it. To cite a classic experiment of Ralph Hefferline of Columbia: A subject is wired to suffer an annoying regular buzz, which can be delayed and finally eliminated if he makes a precise but unlikely gesture, say, by twisting his ankle in a certain way; then it is found that he adjusts more quickly if he is *not* told the method and it is left to his spontaneous twitching than if he is told and tries deliberately to help himself —he adjusts better without conscious control, either the experimenter's or his own.

Technological modesty, fittingness, is not negative. It is the ecological wisdom of cooperating with Nature rather than trying to master her. (The personification of "Nature" is linguistic wisdom.) A well-known example is the long-run superiority of partial pest control in farming by using biological rather than chemical deterrents. The living defenders work harder, at the right moment, and with more pinpointed targets. But let me give another example because it is so lovely (I have forgotten the name of my informant): A tribe in Yucatan educates its children to identify and pull up all weeds in the region; then what is left is a garden of useful plants that have chosen to be there and that now thrive.

In the life sciences there are at present two opposite trends in methodology. The rule is still to increase experimental intervention; but there is also a considerable revival of old-fashioned naturalism, mainly watching and thinking, with very modest intervention. Thus, in medicine, there is new diagnostic machinery, new drugs, spectacular surgery; but there is also a new respect for family practice with a psychosomatic background, and a strong push, among young doctors and students, for a social-psychological and sociological approach, aimed at prevention and building up resistance. In psychology, the operant conditioners multiply and refine their machinery to give maximum control of the organism and the environment (I have not heard of any dramatic discoveries, but likely I don't understand); on the other hand, the most interesting psychology in recent years has certainly come from animal naturalists: studies of the pecking order, territoriality, learning to control aggression, language of the bees, overcrowding among rats, communication of dolphins.

On a fair judgment, both contrasting approaches give positive results. The logical scientific problem that arises is, What is there in the nature of things that makes a certain method, or even moral attitude, work well or poorly in a given case? This question is not much studied. Every scientist seems to know what *the* scientific method is.

"In the pure glow of molecular biology," says Barry Commoner, "studying the biology of sewage is a dull and distasteful exercise hardly worth the attention of a modern biologist. [But] the systems which are at risk in the environment are natural and because they are natural, complex. For this reason they are not readily approached by the atomistic methodology which is so characteristic of much of modern biological research. Any new basic knowledge which is expected to elucidate environmental biology, and guide our efforts to cope with the balance of nature, must be relevant to the natural biological systems which are the arena in which these problems exist."

Another contrast of style, extremely relevant at present, is that between Big Science and old-fashioned shoe-string science. There is plenty of research, with corresponding technology, that can be done only by Big Science; yet much, and perhaps most, of science will always be shoestring science, for which it is absurd to use the fancy and expensive equipment that has gotten to be the fashion.

Consider urban medicine. The problem, given a shortage of doctors and facilities, is how to improve the level of mass health, the vital statistics, and yet to practice medicine which aims at the maximum possible health for each person. Perhaps the most efficient use of Big Science technology for the general health would be to have compulsory biennial checkups, as we inspect cars, for early diagnosis and to forestall chronic conditions and their accumulating costs. But up to now, Dr. Michael Halberstam cautions me, mass diagnosis has not paid off as much as hoped. For this an excellent machine would be a total diagnostic bus that would visit the neighborhoods—as we do chest X-rays. It could be designed by Bell Lab, for instance. On the other hand, for actual treatment and especially for convalescence, the evidence seems to be that small personalized hospitals are best. And to revive family practice, maybe the right idea is to offer a doctor a splendid suite in a public housing project. Here, big corporations might best keep out of it.

It is fantastically expensive to provide and run a hospital bed; yet very many of the beds (up to a third?) are occupied by cases, e.g. tonsillectomies, that could better be dealt with at home if conditions are good, or in tiny infirmaries on each street.

Our contemporary practice makes little sense. We have expensive technology stored in specialists' offices and big hospitals which is unavailable for mass use in the neighborhoods; yet every individual, even if he is quite rich, finds it almost impossible to get attention for himself as an individual whole organism in his setting. He is sent from specialist to specialist and exists as a bag of symptoms and a file of test scores.

In automating, there is an analogous dilemma of how to cope with masses of people and get economies of scale without losing the individual at great consequent human and economic cost. A question of immense importance for the immediate future is, Which functions should be automated or organized to use business machines, and which should not? This question also is not getting asked, and the present disposition is that the sky is the limit for extraction, refining, manufacturing, processing, packaging, transportation, clerical work, ticketing, transactions, information retrieval, recruitment, middle management, evaluation, diagnosis, instruction, and even research and invention. Whether the machines can do all these kinds of jobs and more is partly an empirical question, but it also partly depends on what is meant by doing a job. Very often, for example in college admissions, machines are acquired for putative economies (which do not eventuate), but the true reason is that an overgrown and overcentralized organization cannot be administered without them. The technology conceals the essential trouble, perhaps that there is no community of the faculty and that students are treated like things. The function is badly performed, and finally the system breaks down anyway. I doubt that enterprises in which interpersonal relations are very important are suited to much programming.

But worse, what can happen is that the real function of an enterprise is subtly altered to make it suitable for the mechanical system. (For example, "information retrieval" is taken as an adequate replacement for critical scholarship.) Incommensurable factors, individual differences, local context, the weighing of evidence, are quietly overlooked, though they may be of the essence. The system, with its subtly transformed purposes, seems to run very smoothly, it is productive, and it is more and more out of line with the nature of things and the real problems. Meantime the system is geared in with other enterprises of society, and its products are taken at face value. Thus, major public policy may depend on welfare or unemployment statistics which, as they are tabulated, are not about anything real. In such a case, the particular system may not break down; the whole society may explode.

I need hardly point out that American society is peculiarly liable to the corruption of inauthenticity. Busily producing phony products, it lives by public relations, abstract ideals, front politics, show-business communications, mandarin credentials. It is preeminently overtechnologized. And computer technologists especially suffer the euphoria of being in a new and rapidly expanding field. It is so astonishing that a robot can do the job at all, or seem to do it, that it is easy to blink at the fact that he is doing it badly or isn't really doing quite the job.

iv

The current political assumption is that scientists and inventors, and even social scientists, are value-neutral, but that their discoveries are "applied" by those who make decisions for the nation. Counter to this, I have been insinuating into the reader's mind a kind of Jeffersonian democracy or guild socialism (I am really an anarchist), namely, that scientists and inventors and other workmen are responsible for the uses of the work they do, and they ought to be competent to judge these uses and have a say in deciding them. They usually are competent. To give a poignant example, Ford assembly-line workers, according to Harvey Swados who worked with them, are accurately critical of the glut of cars, but they have no way to vent their dissatisfaction with their useless occupation except to leave nuts and bolts to rattle in the body.

My bias is also pluralistic. Instead of the few national goals of a few decision-makers, I think that there are many goods in many activities of life, and many professions and other interest groups each with its own criteria and goals, that must be taken into account. It is better not to organize too tightly, or there is unnecessary trouble. A society that distributes power widely is superficially conflictful but fundamentally stable.

Research and development ought to be widely decentralized, the national fund for them being distributed through thousands of centers of initiative and decision. This would not be chaotic. We seem to have forgotten that for four hundred years, Western science majestically progressed with no central direction whatever, yet with exquisite international coordination, little duplication, almost nothing getting lost, in constant communication despite slow facilities. The reason was simply that all scientists wanted to get on with the same enterprise of testing the boundaries of knowledge, and they relied on one another.

And it is noteworthy that something similar holds also in invention and innovation, even in recent decades when there has been such a concentration of funding and apparent concentration of opportunity. The majority of big advances have still come from independents, partnerships, and tiny companies (evidence published by the Senate Subcommittee on Antitrust and Monopoly, May 1965). To name a few, jet engines, xerography, automatic transmission, cellophane, air conditioning, quick freeze, antibiotics, and tranquilizers. Big technological teams must have disadvantages that outweigh their advantages—such as lack of single-mindedness, poor communications, awkward scheduling, not to speak of enormous overhead and offices full of idle people or people doing busywork. Naturally, big corporations have taken over the innovations, but the Senate evidence is that 90 percent of the government subsidy has gone for last-stage development for production, which they ought to have paid for out of their own pockets.

In the exploding technology, a remarkable phenomenon has been that enterprising young fellows split off from big firms, form small companies of their own, and succeed mightily. A recent study of such cases along Route 128 shows that the salient characteristic of the independents is that their fathers were independents!

We now have a theory that we have learned to learn, and that we can program technical progress, directed by a central planning board. But this doesn't make it so. The essence of the new still seems to be that nobody has thought of it before, and the ones who get ideas are those in direct contact with the work. *Too precise* a preconception of what is wanted discourages creativity more than it channels it; and bureaucratic memoranda from distant directors don't help. This is especially true when, as at present, so much of the preconception of what is wanted comes from desperate political anxiety in emergencies. Solutions that emerge from such an attitude rarely strike out on new paths, but rather repeat traditional thinking with new gimmicks; they tend to compound the problem. A priceless advantage of widespread decentralization is that it engages more minds, and more mind, instead of a few panicky (or greedy) corporate minds.

A homespun advantage of small groups, according to the Senate testimony, is that co-workers can talk to one another, without schedules, reports, clock-watching, and face-saving.

An important hope in decentralizing science is to develop knowledgeable citizens, and provide not only a bigger pool of scientists and inventors but also a public better able to protect itself and know how to judge the enormous budgets asked for. The safety of the environment is too important to be left to scientists, even ecologists. During the last decades of the nineteenth century and the first decade of the twentieth, the heyday of public faith in the beneficent religion of science and invention, say, from Pasteur and Huxley to Edison and the Wright Brothers, philosophers of science had a vision of a "scientific way of life," one in which people would be objective, respectful of evidence, accurate, free of superstition and taboo, immune to irrational authority, experimental. All would be well, is the impression one gets from Thomas Huxley, if everybody knew the splendid ninth edition of the *Encyclopedia Britannica* with its articles by Darwin and Clerk Maxwell. Veblen put his faith in the modesty and matter-of-factness of Engineers to govern. Louis Sullivan and Frank Lloyd Wright spoke for an austere functionalism and respect for the nature of materials and industrial processes. Patrick Geddes thought that new technology would finally get us out of the horrors of the Industrial Revolution and produce good communities. John Dewey devised a system of education to rear pragmatic and experimental citizens who would be at home in the new technological world, rather than estranged from it. Now fifty years later, we are in the swamp of a scientific and technological environment, and there are more scientists alive, etc., etc. But the mention of the "scientific way of life" seems like black humor.

Many of those who have grown up since 1945 and have never seen any other state of science and technology, assume that rationalism itself is totally evil and dehumanizing. It is probably more significant than we like to think that they go in for astrology and the Book of Changes, as well as inducing psychedelic dreams by technological means. Jacques Ellul, a more philosophic critic than the hippies, tries to show that technology is necessarily over-controlling, standardizing, and voraciously inclusive, so that there is no place for freedom. But I doubt that any of this is intrinsic to science and technology. The crude history has been, rather, that they have fallen, willingly, under the dominion of money and power. Like Christianity or communism, the scientific way of life has never been tried. And, as in the other two cases, we have gotten the horrors of abusing a good idea, *corruptio optimi pessima*.

V

To satisfy the March 4th dissenters, to break the military industrial corporations and alter the priorities of the budget, would be to restructure the American economy almost to a revolutionary extent. But to meet the historical crisis of science at present, for science and technology to become prudent, ecological, and decentralized, requires a change that is even more profound; it would be a kind of religious transformation. Yet there is nothing untraditional in what I have proposed; prudence, ecology, and decentralization are indeed the high tradition of science and technology. Thus, the closest analogy I can think of is the Protestant Reformation, liberation from the Whore of Babylon and return to the pure faith.

Science has long been the chief orthodoxy of modern times and has certainly been badly corrupted, but the deepest flaw of the affluent societies that has alienated the young is not, finally, their imperialism, economic injustice, or racism, bad as these are, but their nauseating phoniness, triviality, and wastefulness, the cultural and moral scandal that Luther found when he went to Rome in 1510. And precisely science, which should have been the wind of truth to clear the air, has polluted the air, helped to brainwash, and provided weapons for war. I doubt that most young people today have even heard of the ideal of the dedicated researcher, truculent and incorruptible, and unrewarded, for instance the "German scientist" that Sinclair Lewis described in *Arrowsmith*. Such a figure is no longer believable. I don't mean, of course, that he doesn't exist; there must be thousands such, just as there were good priests in 1510.

The analogy to the Reformation is even more exact if we consider the school system, from educational toys and Head Start up through the universities. This system is manned by the biggest horde of monks since the time of Henry VIII. It is the biggest industry in the country. I have heard the estimate that 40 percent of the national product is in the Knowledge Business. It is mostly hocus pocus. Yet the delusory belief of parents in this institution is quite absolute, and school diplomas are in fact the only entry to licensing and hiring for every kind of job. The abbots of this system are the chiefs of Science, e.g., the National Science Foundation, who talk about reform but work to expand the school budgets, step up the curriculum, and inspire the endless catechism of tests.

These abuses are international, as the faith is. For instance, there is no essential difference between the military-industrial or the school systems of the Soviet Union and the United States. There are important differences in way of life and standard of living, but the abuses of technology are very similar—pollution, excessive urbanization, destruction of the biosphere, weaponry, and disastrous foreign aid. Our protesters naturally single out our own country, and the United States is the most powerful country, but the corruption we are speaking of is not specifically American, nor even capitalist; it is a disease of modern times.

But the analogy is to the Reformation; it is not to primitive Christianity or some other primitivism, the abandonment of technological civilization. There is indeed much talk about the doom of western civilization, and a few Adamites actually do retire into the hills, but for the great mass of mankind, and myself, that's not where it's at. Despite all the movements for national liberation, there is not the slightest interruption to the universalizing of Western civilization, including most of its delusions, into the so-called Third World. (If the atom bombs go off, however?)

Naturally, the exquisitely interesting question is whether or not this Reformation will occur, how to make it occur, against the entrenched worldwide power that is also continually aggrandizing itself. I don't know. In my analogy I have deliberately chosen the date 1510, Luther in Rome, rather than 1517 when, in the popular story, he nailed his Theses to the cathedral door; and this book will keep returning to present dilemmas and contradictory signs of the future. For instance, the new professional and technological class is more and more entangled in the work, statuses, and rewards of the system; yet this same class—often the same people—is more and more protestant. On the other hand, the dissident young, who are unequivocally and hell-bent for radical change, are so alienated that they often seem to be simply irrelevant to the underlying issues of modern times; they care only for their "gut" issues. The monks keep "improving" the schools and getting bigger budgets to do so, but the schools are in trouble and there is no end of it in sight. The interlocking of technologies and other institutions makes it almost impossible to reform policy in any part; yet this very interlocking creates a resonance and a chain-reaction if a determined group—even a determined individual—is indeed insistent. In the face of overwhelmingly collective operations, such as space exploration, the average man must feel that small or local effort is worthless and there is no possible administration but the State; yet there is everywhere a surge of populism and community action, as if people were determined to have local liberty, even if it makes no sense. A mighty empire is stood off by a band of peasants, and *neither* can win; this is even more remarkable than if David beat Goliath. It means that neither principle is historically adequate. It is because of impasses and dilemmas like these that I think we are on the eve of a transformation of conscience.

Chapter 2

i

Space exploration has so far been an epitome of the grandeur and misery of Man in our times. It presents us with all the dilemmas.

I am writing this chapter in July 1969, when the two men have just walked on the Moon, and five hundred million televiewers have watched it. Surely this is mankind being great at several of our best things, exploring the unknown, making ingenious contraptions, cooperating with a will to do it, drawing on the accumulation of culture and history, whether we think of the equations of Galileo, Kepler, and Newton, or of the roving Polynesians, Vikings, Columbus, and Magellan. And we have satisfied our lust to see at a distance: the pictures a second later were as sensational as the voyage. People do beat all! When the first Sputnik flew on October 4, 1957, I wrote the following sonnet—and it is so:

> A new thing with heavenly motion made by us
> flies in the sky, it is passing every hour
> signalling in our language. What a power
> of thought and hand has launched this marvelous
> man-made moon, and suddenly the gorgeous
> abyss lies open, as you spring a door
> to enter and visit where no man before
> ever came.

It is a mysterious
moment when one crosses a threshold
and "Have I been invited?" is my doubt.
Yes, for our wish and wonder from of old
and how we patiently have puzzled out
the laws of entry, warrant we have come
into the great hall as a man comes home.

This combination of itching exploration and complicated machinery is, of course, a peculiarly Western mask of man, Faustian man. Bodhisattvas have tended to go on inner space-time voyages, with psychological technology. But ours *is* a way of being that we have invented/discovered; it is how we have appointed ourselves and are. In our times it is a worldwide way, which the Orient and Africa also identify with; and we are going to continue it, however arduous, till we revert to barbarism or annihilation.

To attempt to belittle this event, as some of the radicals have tried, is to miss the worldwide public feeling. When Eldridge Cleaver, the exiled black leader, calls it a circus, it is understandable polemical spite. When Noam Chomsky, the linguist, calls it a circus, it seems to me to be rather inexcusable snobbery, as if only professors at M.I.T. have a right to play noble and exciting games. The "coverage" is simply the American style: since the age of Jackson, the Americans have tried to do everything, good, bad, or indifferent, in a glare of publicity; and the Moon reporting has been quite decent. Dissident scientists have complained that it was enough to send up a package of instruments, without so much expense and fuss. They don't seem to understand that people are excited by a new horizon for existence, not a file of data for research; and we don't believe, or don't want to believe, that abstract calculations are as true as experience, however naïve. And I don't think that the economic priority has been as mistaken as the radicals have unanimously claimed. Since science is our religion, these are our cathedrals. A part of living well is to waste money that you can't afford on big excitement, curiosity, and a better level of chatter. It is strange how often radicals lose their common sense when they talk politics. To tell a child or a man that he can't have ice cream or whiskey because there are starving Armenians is to be so serious as to deserve not to be taken seriously. And in a matter like this, which embodies so many ideals and even humane imperatives, to be grudging is to be petty.

There is nothing ironical in the fact that we can land on the Moon but can't move traffic, feed the hungry, build housing, or educate a child. NASA can't make an epigram or a metaphor either. All these take different powers of soul; and it is politically a disaster to try to play one good against another, for people will stick to what they do value. Consider the exquisite care for safety in our space program —it is astounding that there was only one accident that cost lives. If there had been the slightest hint of sacrificing a life to go to the Moon, there would have been universal outrage, as there was when the little monkey died in orbit. Yet we ruthlessly destroy people on battlefields, in jails, in slums. But it is pointless to call this hypocrisy, for it's not. In some things we have learned to be human; in other things, we are stupid and all too human.

Political economists say that we have to judge the Moon adventure as part of the whole social picture, in terms of comparative importance and rational balance of costs. If they are unfriendly, they speak of decaying cities; if they are friendly, they calculate the spin-off of useful innovations. No, not in borderline cases like this. No good Samaritan, or artist, or kid in love, or guerrilla ever judges with that kind of balance. In my opinion, to have commanded the Moon landing was the only action of John Kennedy that rightly fitted his adolescent mentality, and therefore it had grace. Contrast the inappropriateness of his adolescent poker-playing during the Cuban missile crisis or his adolescent moral cowardice during the Bay of Pigs. It's too bad that he didn't live to bask in the Moon glory.

i i

Accept the Moon enterprise in its own terms, however, as something unquestionably to be done and worth doing —there have been things so wrong in its context and style that it is impossible to be happy. From the beginning, the race with the Russians has been degrading—competitiveness was also part of the personality of John Kennedy. Going to the Moon and the planets is too big, too scientifically important, too historic, too dependent on all mankind, and too fraught with future for all mankind, to have gotten entangled in the Cold War, propaganda, prestige. The secrecy and nationalism have gone counter to the tradition of Western science and have added to the current degradation of science. I have been surprised that the scientists did not protest it more concertedly; but it seems appallingly obvious, for instance, from the refusal to allow a United Nations flag to be carried, that except for the Cold War Congress would never have voted the money. Was this really the sentiment of the Americans (or the Russians)? I wonder what a poll about international cooperation would have shown. In our government's official rhetoric, e.g. the statements of the astronauts on various occasions, we have indeed been considerably less chauvinistic than the Russians, but the history does not bear out our universalistic tone. On the other hand, bad as the situation is, we must remember that when Columbus, returning from his first voyage, put in at Lisbon, the king of Portugal plotted to banish him, his crew, his ship, and his parrots from the face of the earth before the news got abroad.

The race has been especially unfortunate since space exploration is a natural bridge for international coming together, like the Geophysical Year, the World Health Organization, and UNICEF. There has been enough sentiment for internationalism to generate the U.N. treaty barring annexation and military use. And one has the wan hope that to put cooperative effort and capital into vast international activities may drain energy from the insane aggrandizement of the sovereign powers. Perhaps now that the first flush of the race is over, we can revert to that idea. There is a good proposal before the U.N. to launch an orbiting platform for the use of all nations. Maybe the Americans and Russians will back it simply because they are going broke.

The military danger speaks for itself. The Pentagon and our military-industrial corporations and the military powers in the Kremlin have boosted and controlled the space ventures every step of the way. Every part of the technology is potentially a weapon. The first Sputnik itself grew out of the development of nuclear missiles. The satellites are used for spying, and we have even toyed with building an armed platform, in violation of the U.N. treaty. The brute fact is this: If the Russians can hit Venus at thirty million miles and we can photograph Mars at a similar distance, we had better stop talking about Defense.

We thus have the ambiguity that very many people are ingenuously excited about exploring space, and the mass of mankind seem to think it's right; and many fine but craft-idiot scientists are so eager to do this work that they don't care about its auspices. Nevertheless, the funding, organization, and technology are inextricably tangled in the war machine. Needless to say, the space statements of the President all have to do with peace and universal brotherhood—this *is* hypocrisy, unless it is simply, as Disraeli said of Gladstone, that he and his conscience are accomplices. On the other hand, the public coverage has stuck with remarkable purity to the adventure, the wonder, the ingenuity, with almost no martial or imperial overtones: this *is* the way people want it.

Partly because of the military auspices—but of course it is the symptom of a deeper disease in our country—the astronauts, the *personae* of the enterprise, have been strangely homogeneous, men in their late thirties, with combat records and 2.2 children, from small towns, and so forth. Naturally one cannot be too careful when there is so much risk of persons and equipment, but I should guess that a draft-resister, a Puerto Rican dropout, a farm mother of five, or even a queer might be trained for the job equally well. The Russians seem to have been able to collect more various and colorful types.

i i i

But there is another aspect to these events more disturbing than any of the above: the overwhelming collectivity of the enterprise. This does not leave a bad taste in the mouth, for it is in the nature of things and has its own kind of beauty; but it is frightening for the future. One can think away the militarism from space exploration—and one way or another we will have to get rid of it in this generation, or we are done for—but the collectivity is inherent in Big Science, and if mankind has a future, how to cope with it?

From the beginning a dozen years ago, one had the strong whiff of it: they were numerous and busy as ants, on the steppe and at Cape Canaveral, mounting, aiming, and firing their gun, with a single-minded social purpose to which they willingly gave themselves—it was the willingness and enthusiasm that made them different from industrial masses.* In July 1969, it takes your breath away: the thousands upon thousands of machinists, construction workers, and clerical staff and grease-monkeys and professors and technicians and drivers, infallibly interlocking, going through hundreds of tryouts in order to get everything by rote, timed by the computer. The countdown is

---

* I find in my notebook in 1957: "The busy single-minded men, on the steppe and at Cape Canaveral, in their hundreds and thousands, taking their positions, springing into action. Bright-eyed and hot, fraught with the future of an immediate enterprise, but otherwise blind and in darkness. They frighten me. Also I love them and the thought of them gives me courage. They are ants, not vermin as in my other disgusted fantasy of human beings. I know their intelligent purpose. What frightens me is how their concentration on the enterprise, mutually supporting one another, allows them to cut loose from guilt and resentment, but also from love and compassion."— *Five Years*, Winter 1957–58, Section v.

by seconds and lasts for days. And the other armies of TV teams and laboratories of scientists with their lasers, seismographs, and set-ups to measure radioactivity all accurately plugged into it. And five hundred million watchers.

I do not mean that the workmen are robotized. They cannot be, or there would be blunders and catastrophe, for machines are not quite that bright. On the contrary, they look alert, attentive. I say "like ants" to indicate a superorganism, but they are individuals—as probably the ants are too, if we knew. And the five hundred million do not seem brainwashed, nor even "passive" in any ugly sense, but just docile, willing to be instructed.

Yet there is a terrible loss of flashing spirit and personality. For instance, I don't know anything about the architectonic designers, hardly one or two names. In this set-up it would not be right for them to take a bow. According to Professor Zacharias, James Webb, the administrator up to 1968, "orchestrated the activities of thousands of companies, tens of thousands of engineers and scientists, and hundreds of thousands of other participants"—a handsome duchy, but I didn't recall his name. Von Braun was enthusiastically chaired on the shoulders of some of the staff; he has not been invited to address the Congress. The rejected loner Goddard can exist only as the name of a NASA space center. With the best will in the world—and oh, they have the will!—the TV teams cannot make the astronauts look like anything but middle-aged tame boys, though Neil Armstrong did rouse my fellow feeling by his uneasiness at putting his foot down, in that airless world and blinding sunlight, on the ground that might sink beneath him. In this enterprise we certainly seem to see Teilhard de Chardin's transcendent Noösphere, the human super-mind, in operation; and it does not rouse in me the spiritual eros that it used to arouse in him. Except for my unhappiness at the militarism, I willingly identify as a man with men walking on the moon, but I do not feel prideful joy, for my colleagues, my boys, my team; and I guess that my muted satisfaction has been pretty general.

The collectivity is inherent in the enterprise, and that is acceptable since the purpose is not stupid and the people are not coerced. Nevertheless, as an anarchist and a psychologist, I am quite convinced that this kind of social organization, habituation to rote, and controlled environment is not, in a big way, viable. If it becomes universal, no child will learn anything, the culture will become Byzantine, and civilization itself will become brittle and break. What seems to be a triumph could be the beginning of the end of the road. The history of civilization, both Western and Oriental, has consisted of visitations of spirit, in individuals and communities, which have then enlightened mankind. I do not believe that the collective will be visited by Spirit, although I know it bloweth where it listeth.

Consider it in the future and in the present. We must and will pursue these explorations. Hopefully we will colonize, as Buckminster Fuller thinks and urges, and he has been a wise predicter. As always in the past, the culture and style of the colonies will depend on the character of the colonists and the organization of the colonization. To give an off-beat example, the Hawaiians had a brutal theology, a rigid feudalism, and a rudimentary culture compared with the graceful Polynesia that they left behind; but what would you expect from bully rovers with ants in their pants, who astonishingly crossed two and three thousand miles of open sea to settle? Inevitably, all the present talk about colonizing the Moon and planets centers on mining and cryogenic operations carried on by computerized personnel, and of outlets for the surplus population that we cannot cope with here, like the convicts that were sent to Georgia and Australia. It has happened in history that the colonies have sometimes become far more important than the mother countries.

What must be the present effect on the man on the street? These great achievements will justifiably make the fashion in behavior and speech—ow! "Roger" "Over," "All systems go," "Houston, I'm on the Porch." But they are likely also, not quite so justifiably, to make people believe that there can be no great achievement except in this collective style, organized from top down; no science but Big Science; no thought and culture except plugged into the

Noösphere. As the Boston *Globe* put it in an editorial: much as they like the hippies, and much as they morally agreed with the student radicals, to go to the Moon you've got to be pretty square, shape up, and do your lessons.

I don't think there is any simple answer to this dilemma. The Boston *Globe* may be right, but as Coleridge said in a similar context, referring to the Industrial Revolution and the Manchester economists, "In order to have [economic] citizens, you must first be sure that you have produced men." If this collective enterprise is necessary for the on-going human adventure, we must go with it or commit historical suicide. At the same time, in order to have live people at all, we must multiply all the "anarchist" things: decentralize wherever it is possible, weaken the State, do it yourself, educate to delay socialization. It will not be easy to show the ordinary man that these apparently contrary directions are compatible. Maybe they are institutionally not compatible and we *are* at a dead end.

iv

Esthetically, our great achievement is not epic. (Therefore it has no pedagogic value, especially for adolescents.) Objectively it is as arduous and dangerous and important for the tribe as any epic exploration, battle, or city-founding of the past. But what is lacking is the dual nature that belongs to epic heroism: epic heroes are representative champions of the people, with the virtues specific to carrying out their great tasks, but at the same time they are serious and suffering persons, with a commitment and destiny and often a tragic frailty and doom that are their own. So the epic feelings are admiration and pride, often mixed with pity and fear. But at present, instead of being champions and persons, the agents of great deeds are becoming personnel of the collective.

This has occurred rapidly in the past century. Pasteur was an epic figure; Fleming and Salk have been much less so. Laying the railroad and the cable and digging the Panama Canal were more epic than building the big dams and orbiting Telstar. Going to the Poles was more epic than going to the Moon. Even among professionals, Wright and LeCorbusier were more Architects than their successors have been, and J.J. Thomson, Einstein, and Bohr were more Scientists than their successors have been. No doubt our contemporaries are persons just as forceful and interesting, but there is much less public belief in the relevance of their personalities. Previously, even when deeds were essentially corporate, people personalized them; now, even when deeds are very much the work of individual genius, people regard them as corporate.

There is no less hunger for personal identification. But the arduous and dangerous deeds of individuals are taken as romantic or eccentric rather than as epic and important. These can range from Thor Heyerdahl's efforts to prove that the Polynesians and Egyptians could cross the oceans with primitive means, to aging Mr. Chichester sailing alone around the world in a ketch and proving that there will always be an England—he was properly knighted for it—to the gentleman who recently crossed Lake Michigan in a bathtub and proved that there is an America. The agents of such exploits become celebrities.

There *is* identification with the Moon landing, but it is not with its champions or model heroes. My guess is that astronauts are celebrities for only a few days, because it is not felt that there is anything in *them*. Rather, the identification is massive, a social bond, quasi-religious, expressing how we are in the world. It will appear most strikingly as a style of Space toys, successor to the trains and cars, bought by those over thirty for those under ten. We have added explosive fire to force and speed. Rockets are guns as well as flying machines.

To a bright seventeen-year-old, however, I find upon questioning him, not only the heroes but even the exploit, the Moon landing, is unimportant. It was talked to death beforehand, he says, there was no surprise. We learned everything that went into it in high school. What would be surprising? Something proving Tarot cards. (!) The Moon itself is of no interest, it's only a way station. It was never remarkable to him that we got a photograph of the other side of the Moon. Would a voyage to Mars be more interesting? No, nowhere in the same old solar system; maybe to one of the stars. What about Kepler and Newton? Isn't it remarkable that everything, the escape velocity, the curves of the orbits, the one-sixth gravity, and all, is just as they said? No, that's science; science always works out; that's what's wrong with it. He himself is going to major in mathematics and physics at Dartmouth.

Chapter 3

On March 4, I myself was invited to dissent at Rockefeller University in New York City. Since I am not a scientist, and competent scientists had covered the abuses in their special fields, I thought of discussing something more philosophical, the general history of the relationship of science, technology, and social needs, as compared and contrasted with our present situation. I am not a historian, but I did the best I could, traversing two thousand years in twenty minutes.

Greek science, as epitomized by Aristotle, I said, made a dumb-bunny matter-of-fact distinction between two kinds of knowledge: watching and reasoning about what you saw, and intelligently making or doing something. These were the "theoretical" and "practical" sciences.

Being good watchers and reasoners, the Greeks did excellent analyses of motion, elements, heavenly bodies, biological functions, and natural history. But they had poor apparatus and they did not experiment, so though their philosophical descriptions are still useful, there is little enduring value in their theoretical sciences as sciences. (An exception is Greek psychology, which still has a lot of vitality for us, perhaps because in this field they got as close to the data as we do, and they had fewer misconceptions to start with.) Their shortcoming was not that they were not empirical; their observations were good, and Aristotle's

Topics touches many bases of experimental method like Mill's canons, but there is little actual experimental intervention.

In making and doing, on the other hand, the Greeks were intelligently experimental through and through, more than we are, perhaps because they had simpler conditions to cope with. After twenty-five hundred years, we still draw continually on their practical sciences, politics, rhetoric, medicine, ethics, pedagogy, poetics, architecture and city planning. These studies were entirely pragmatic. Immediate purpose was intrinsic to the study, the method, and the scientist. They were like arts and crafts, *technai,* and the technician was responsible for both the purpose and the execution. The scientists were the directors; and the scale of operations made this possible—Athens had perhaps a hundred thousand people.

They did not yet have to make the more learned distinction between natural and moral philosophy. No studies were value-neutral, whether theoretical or practical. The watching sciences each had a peculiar excellence that made it worthwhile explained in the first paragraph of the treatise; and in general, disinterested study was itself good and liberating—for free adult males, whose chief social activity was leisure. Theory was not practical only in that there was nothing to make or do.

In the watching sciences, Aristotle was not fussy about looking for "final causes" or purposes, a notion that really applies to making and doing. Sometimes he neglected to mention them. Other times he resorted to formulas like "An animal has its purpose in itself" or "An element seeks its own kind of place." Conversely, except among Platonists, there was almost no tendency for pure theory to give principles to practice. Making and doing determined their own methods and goals.

There was no such thing as objective social science. Human beings were studied for their purposes or one's own purposes. And by and large (though Plato again reasoned otherwise), there were many goods, of many activities, implemented by many practical sciences. Unlike later moral philosophy, there was little disposition to organize the many purposes to one or a few goods. Thus in his *Ethics,* Aristotle quickly divides good life into having friends, health, luck, money, courage, temperance, prudence, justice; and he studies how to form habits that might produce these advantages. All human purposes cohered in the *polis,* but this was not a Sovereign with its own will like our States. The constitution of a *polis* was how the many interests were actually related in a region, its functional organization. Where a single will dominated with *its* interest, it was called a tyranny.

As it passed through Hellenistic and Roman times, when there were only tyrannies and finally the Sovereign Empire, the behavioral distinction of watching versus doing gradually hardened into the "objective" distinction of natural and moral philosophy. The difference was now not in a man's approach, the kind of activity he happened to be engaged in, but in the subject matter, natural affairs versus human affairs. And to think philosophically now became a specialist activity rather than a quality of every activity. Thus, there could in principle be purely theoretical ethics without doing anything, or practical physics, e.g. engineering, without any moral purpose. There began to be "disciplines" and "applied science."

During the Roman Empire, this seems to have worked out as follows. The busy Romans were not so good at disinterested watching and thinking, and the natural sciences made slower progress, though there were great men like Archimedes. On the other hand, the rapidly advancing physical technology, e.g. engineering, was hardly philosophized at all, as either natural or moral philosophy. It was plain know-how, used by those in power; the books were manuals.

But some moral sciences—jurisprudence and, increasingly, Christian morality—became highly principled and systematic. The government of men in an expanding empire was serious business. These studies were aimed at regulating human behavior and were less experimental in spirit than the Greek practical sciences. We still use them for regulation. The more liberal moral sciences became otiose. Politics became the theory of the (often-changing) status quo. Rhetoric became ornamental. Ethics became personal duty. And pedagogy, the chief philosophical study among the Greeks, almost vanished from sight; one made citizens not by growing them but by imposing the laws.

As in any centralized social engineering, the many goods tended to be organized into a very few—political *raison d'état* and moral *summum bonum*. Since the warrant for these lofty concepts was not found in ordinary immediate practice and common sense, there developed, much more than among the Greeks, the notion that abstract principles of natural philosophy determined right behavior. Among the naturalistic Epicureans, the lesson of cosmology was to withdraw from political life. Among the Stoics, climactically with Marcus Aurelius, the lesson was to enact the immutable laws of the Cosmos, which were rather transparently a projection of imperial institutions. Among Gnostics, Neo-Platonists, and Christians, right behavior became an imitation of metaphysical history.

The engineering was imperial civil service in style and content. For a Roman technician, it must have been "value-neutral"—he was not responsible for the organization or use of his work.

In the high Middle Ages, the relation of natural and moral philosophy and technology were again very different. The ancient theoretical sciences became, if anything, still more static, and were too bookish; instead of observing, one read about other people's observations, and progress depended mainly on getting better Greek and Arabic texts. But the organization of society was pluralistic and pragmatic; the moral sciences came alive, and in the physical sciences, there began to be widespread experimentation.

In the heterogeneous political structure of feudalism, national states, city states, municipal councils, craft guilds, trade associations, the international church, and the ghost of the international empire, there was a thriving moral philosophy and law, inventive and probing. Today, in every kind of moral inquiry, religious or secular, the medieval analyses reappear, in commercial transactions, craft regulation, sexual morality, rules of war, university polity and privilege, discussions of sovereignty and legitimacy.

In form, medieval moral philosophy was apparently

systematic rather than experimental, aiming at the *summum bonum* of salvation. But in the great variety of occasions and jurisdictions, casuistry made moral inquiry concrete and pragmatic. Scholasticism and legalism provided a consensual language that made thought precise, rather than stifling it. Arts and crafts, technology, were, like all other activities, personal, moral, and responsible, e.g. in determining quality and just price and in guild and building-gang organization. Indeed, the free-city guilds were the closest we have yet come to workers' management.

Onto this pluralistic and pragmatic scene appeared the dramatic new force of experimental science; but the opposite of our situation, it was in the context of prudence and morals. *Prima facie,* experimentation was a making and doing, a branch of moral philosophy, liable to moral judgment and not simply a means of knowing; nor were its findings acceptable in style to orthodox academic natural philosophy. One important source of experimentation was the arts and crafts revived or newly invented by self-directed artisans who were both highly cooperative and highly competitive, producing for their own purposes and judging what they were doing, an excellent set-up for learning new science without bookish scientific preconceptions, and strictly prudential.

Another important source of experiment was alchemy and other magic. And here, just because magical tampering with matter could be random, explosive in results, and not bound to definite uses, it was rightly recognized that it was dangerous, so that a sharp distinction was made between white and black magic. To experiment, one was supposed to be a good Christian with virtuous motives.

Just because all science was regarded as immediately practical, however, there was censorship.

In academic philosophy there was *libertas philosophandi,* freedom to debate; but inevitably any radically new truth, whether given by experiment, wider-ranging observation, or better texts, would alter Natural Law and have disruptive moral effects, as well as being cosmological heresy. Then, to protect themselves from suppression, the Averroists, who did teach new natural doctrines, invented

the fateful argument that scientific truth was neutral, it had
no consequences in social or moral practice or religious
belief. Some—and I agree—have interpreted this argument
of the Dual Truth as a deception: the Averroists did have
a moral purpose, to undermine the orthodoxy. Others say
that they held the ultra-modern position, that science is indeed indifferent to practice; but I cannot conceive of an
ancient or medieval having such a view.

In the succeeding centuries, experimentation became
an essential method of natural philosophy and destroyed
the ancient distinction between watching and doing. During the heroic age of modern science, and indeed well into
the nineteenth century, this had the reasonable conse-
quence that natural philosophy was considered especially
subject to moral judgment; it could be beneficent or dangerous—it was certainly not value-neutral.

Discarding the Averroist pretension that no truth of
reality followed from scientific discoveries, the natural philosophers progressively undermined orthodox cosmology,
biology, and psychology, often with revolutionary intent
and often suffering for it. And their success created the expectation that the same methods of scientific analysis and
experiment would solve all political and social problems as
well, which became one of the ideas of the French Revolution, the Rule of Reason. This has not yet proved out. But
more justified in the victory of moralized natural philosophy over the old moral philosophy was the continual useful
cooperation between experimental natural science and
practical arts and crafts, constituting scientific technology.
Sometimes utilitarian problems set the scientists to work,
sometimes scientific discoveries were made independently
and applied to use. But in every field, from medicine to
manufacture, animal husbandry to transportation and communications, the interplay of natural science and technology produced both remarkable discoveries and useful products.

For these two reasons, explaining away the miracles
and destroying the old faith, and producing goods and won-
ders of its own, we can say that natural philosophy itself
eventually became the orthodox faith that everybody be-

lieved in. Correspondingly, scientists and inventors as a class became esteemed and were rewarded.

With the moral success of science, it was now the old moral philosophy that became otiose and academic. Thrown on the defensive, it beat around for a definition of itself to warrant its waning institutional authority. Moral philosophers gave up the arts and crafts as being not part of moral philosophy—in the popular mind, technology became associated with science, though technical studies were still segregated in technical institutes apart from the university. But they desperately distinguished *Naturwissenschaften*, natural sciences, from *Geisteswissenschaften*, spirit sciences (such as politics, pedagogy, fine arts, sociology); these, they claimed, were entirely different in method from experimental natural science. Natural science was value-neutral and determined fact; spirit science embodied values and legislated action.

This conception seemed to be simply reactionary politics, but in my opinion it had two opposite tendencies, as the future was to bear out. On the one hand, it was an attempt to restore legitimacy after the French Revolution and it took advantage of the fact that the rationalistic ideologues had indeed pretended more for human welfare than they could deliver; social institutions could not be mechanistically explained. Also, disastrously, the German natural scientists, as State functionaries in the universities, were willing to affirm that natural science *was* value-neutral—perhaps in order not to be interfered with (but they cut a less sympathetic figure than the Averroists who defended themselves by this pretext when they were *not* being esteemed and rewarded).

On the other hand, the desperate defense of the separate existence of moral philosophy was also a kind of existentialist protest. In the line of Pascal, Kant, Kierkegaard, Bakunin, and Nietzsche, moralists saw that no rational doctrine was close enough to free human experience to dictate morals and politics, and they foresaw that science and scientific technology would become a new established superstition, incalculably dangerous.

At the beginning of the twentieth century, however,

especially in the United States, the difficulties were harmonized by an optimistic pragmatism, the zenith of science as a beneficent religion. On this view, there was no distinction between natural and moral philosophy, and science as a whole was value-laden with human advantages, ends-in-view. Social sciences were objective, no different from natural sciences, but they were also experimental: social scientists actively tried to reform institutions or invent better ones, and thereby made scientific discoveries, just as other scientists did—Comte, Marx, Veblen, Dewey, and others. The natural sciences, too, embodied values. For instance, scientific technology demanded developments like economic democracy. And basic research was valuable in itself as a quality of behavior, honest, humble, discriminating, responsible, cooperative, unprejudiced, experimental, progressive. The scientific attitude included a trust in "naturalness," that Nature provided guidelines for conduct, as in progressive education or in radical or conservative deductions from the theory of evolution. Scientists were a fellowship of independent spirits, collaborating, competing with fair play. Their communication promoted international understanding and peace. Some held that, because of their objectivity, incorruptibility, and social conscience the guild of scientists was competent to govern.

After two world wars and a generation of deterrence, today we have the familiar scene of worldwide militarism and imperialism. In Western countries the scientific orthodoxy is that science is neutral; in Communist countries it theoretically follows the ideology. But in either case, by funding and organization, science and technology are directed to a few, not ideal, national purposes.

Even apart from narrow or dubious goals, however, it is believed that the rationalization and central organization of scientific research make for the most efficient use of scientific resources and allow crash programs to cure cancer and go to the Moon.

Further, there has been a change in the metaphysical status of Science, leading to a kind of ecclesiastical structure. Science used to consist of a large number of forays into the unknown according to the inspiration of individual researchers and using the special methods of the various sciences and schools. Now it is increasingly believed that there is one self-contained and self-correcting system of Science, with a common method and, hopefully, a common language. Most recently, the style has been to try to formulate the different sciences in terms of the theory of computers, which are increasingly ubiquitous. Scientific work is valuable in furthering the progress of the self-contained system of Science. It is value-neutral in the isolation of that system from other activities of life. Scientific knowledge is "applied" to other activities, it does not develop from them; nor is being scientific considered a general excellence of habit or character in other walks of life.

In the United States, scientific technology, linked with basic research in the universities and corporations, is in the ambiguous situation that as science it can pretend to be value-neutral, although it is directed to war and expanding the Gross National Product. Social studies have become the behavioral science, defined as control of behavior, and funded for war and social engineering. What are the purposes to which science is "applied?" A positivism, stemming from Hume's and Kant's astringent criticism but omitting Hume's custom and Kant's morality of freedom, makes the goals of practice a matter of whim or force. The scientific way of life has become an unheard-of concept. "Naturalness" is a slogan of disaffected youth antagonistic to science. Far from governing, scientists and engineers are personnel of corporate systems and are not responsible for the programs they implement. The priorities of these programs neglect essential human needs.

There is scientific secrecy and national rivalry. Because of misdirected research carelessly applied, the whole world is overtechnologized and wrongly technologized. The environment is polluted, the biosphere is damaged, resources are being exhausted, and the human species is in danger of extinction. The inflexible interlocking of technologies results in drastic disruptions if anything goes wrong. Underdeveloped regions are drawn into the same ruinous system of hasty and ill-considered industrialization for political reasons.

Among the mass of mankind, science and scientific technology are rightly regarded with awe; but to many they have come to seem diabolic. New experimentation—in physics, biology, and psychology—arouses dread.

We increasingly protest against this state of affairs, and looking toward the future, we want the following reconstruction:

Technology is a branch of moral philosophy, with the criteria of prudence, efficiency, concern for remote effects, safety, amenity, perspicuity and repairability of machines, caution about interlocking, priorities determined by broad social needs.

For the immediate future there must be simplification of the technical system and cautious application of innovations. A good maxim is to innovate in order to simplify, otherwise very sparingly. In underdeveloped regions, an "intermediate technology" should be devised to suit local resources, skills, and customs, with the aim of eliminating disease, hunger, and drudgery without disrupting the pattern of life.

We must emphasize ecology, study and conserve the complexity and balances of the biosphere and physical environment. We must emphasize psychosomatic and sociological preventive medicine. We must understand that we are part of the natural world and abjure the attitude of mastering it.

Researchers must continue to carry on their free dialogue with the unknown, however risky, because this is our human adventure. But balancing this, scientists and technologists have a political responsibility for the consequences of their work; they must fight for its right use and inform and alert the public.

Social sciences are purposive and activist. The political execution of their social values is part of their scientific problem; otherwise sociologists make studies and nothing happens.

In the funding and organization of research and development, we must decentralize initiative and decision so as to maximize the number of minds and interests involved. The mandarin education system must be revised, to increase the pool of the science-minded and raise the level of competence of the general public to judge and protect itself.

We must dispel the superstition of science. There should be more modesty in its claims and rewards. There are other paths of pursuing happiness, and perhaps they even lead to a kind of truth.

When I finished this speech, there was some applause. My impression was that especially the professors had enjoyed the tour.

At once, however, a young lady militant stood up and demanded in a loud voice, "How can you talk about *that,* when people are being killed in Vietnam?"

"Oh? I thought it might be useful," I faltered, "to show how people in other periods of history set it up in different ways."

"What is the relevance of this pedantry?" she cried. "It's detached scholarship!"

"I *thought* I ended up with a program. Didn't you listen that far?"

"*Program!*" she said scornfully. "By program we mean you *do* something."

I was at a loss—she was really quite wrongheaded—so I became miffed. "Listen, young woman—we have our thing too. We're willing to support the Movement, put up bail money, support Dr. Spock and all, even if we disagree with the tactics. But if you think we're going to repeat your idiotic slogans—If I know better, I'll say so; that's *my* thing."

This was exactly the wrong note, a put-down by pulling age and experience; and at once a young fellow jumped to his feet and came halfway down the aisle. "Why are *you* standing up there and controlling the microphone?" he demanded. "Who gives you the right to lecture at *us,* Senator?"

"You can have the microphone if you want. It's not mine—" I turned to the young chairman, but he was vehemently shaking his head. Maybe it was a different faction.

"Senator" was good.

"Look here, you conceited ape," I said angrily, "take René Dubos there." I pointed to the biologist, my friend, in order to have a local ally on this unfamiliar turf. "For nearly fifty years he has been doing useful work for you—yes, for you—and believe me, the work he is now doing in ecology is maybe just as important as getting rid of the military industrial. Now, are you going to tell him that he has spent his life on garbage?"

They looked at one another. "What's the use of talking to this liberal jerk?" she said, and the row of them noisily walked out.

What was altogether wrong with my rejoinders was that the young people deeply, inwardly, fear that they *are* conceited kids—but they're not, not especially—and this rouses their anxiety. Since I undertake to be thirty-five years older, I ought to be able to handle it better. Also they were right, people are being killed in Vietnam. What they didn't seem to understand was that the only useful thing one *can* do at a talk, in Caspary Auditorium at Rockefeller University, is to make reasonable propositions.

Chapter 4

i

In 1967 I was invited to give a course on "professionalism" at the New School for Social Research in New York. (They were expanding the graduate school and the Dean was beating around for a reason for it.) The class consisted of about twenty-five graduates from all departments.

My bias was the traditional one, that professionals are autonomous men, beholden to the nature of things and the judgment of their peers, and not subject to bosses or bureaucrats but bound by an explicit or implicit oath to benefit their clients and the community. To teach this, I invited seasoned professionals whom I esteemed, a physician, engineer, journalist, architect, humanist scholar. These explained to the students the obstacles that increasingly stand in the way of honest practice and their own life experiences in circumventing them.

To my surprise, the class unanimously rejected my guests. Heatedly and rudely, they called them finks, mystifiers, or deluded. They showed that every profession was co-opted and corrupted by the System, that all significant decisions were made by the power structure and bureaucracy, that professional peer groups were only conspiracies to make more money. All this was importantly true and had, of course, been said by the visitors. Why had the students not heard?

As we explored further, we came to the deeper truth

that the students did not believe that there *were* authentic professions at all. Professionalism was a concept of repressive societies and of "linear thinking" (a notion of McLuhan's). I asked them to envisage any social order they pleased—Mao's, Castro's, some anarchist utopia—and wouldn't there be engineers who knew about materials and stresses and strains? Wouldn't people get sick and need to be treated? Wouldn't there be problems of communication and decisions about the news? No. It was necessary only to be human, they insisted, and all else would follow.

Suddenly I realized that they did not believe there was a nature of things. Or they were not sure of that. There was no knowledge but only the sociology of knowledge. They had learned so well that physical and sociological research is subsidized and conducted for the benefit of the ruling class that they were doubtful that there was such a thing as simple truth, for instance that the table was made of wood—maybe it was a plastic imitation. To be required to know something was a trap by which the young were put down and co-opted. Then I knew that my guests and I could not get through to them. I had imagined that the worldwide student protest had to do with changing political and moral institutions, and I was sympathetic to this. But I now saw that we had to do with a religious crisis. Not only all institutions but all learning had been corrupted by the Whore of Babylon, and there was no longer any salvation to be got from Works.

The irony was that I myself had said this ten years before, in *Growing Up Absurd,* that young people were growing up without a world for them, and therefore they were "alienated," estranged from nature and unable to find their own natures, since we find ourselves by activity in the world. But I had then been thinking of juvenile delinquents and a few of the Beat Generation; and a couple of years later, I indeed noticed and wrote about a "New Spirit," the Movement—the Freedom Rides, the Port Huron Statement of the Students for a Democratic Society with its emphasis on decentralization and "participatory democracy," the Free Speech Movement in Berkeley, the rising resistance to the Vietnam War—all of this made human sense and was not absurd at all. (The magazine for which I wrote "New Spirit" in 1960 refused to print it because, they said, there was no such movement.) But now the alienating circumstances had proved to be too strong, after all; here were absurd graduate students, most of them political activists—the activists seek me out to bug me.

ii

Alienation is a Lutheran concept: "God has turned His face away; things have no meaning; I am estranged in the world." By the time of Hegel the idea was applied to the general condition of rational man with his "objective" sciences and institutions divorced from his "subjectivity," which was, in turn, irrational and impulsive. In his revision of Hegel, Marx explained alienation as the effect of Man's losing his essential nature as a cooperative producer; centuries of exploitation, and, climactically, capitalism, had fragmented his community and robbed him of the means of production. Comte and Durkheim spoke of the weakening of social solidarity, the loss of common faith, the contradiction among norms, so that people lost their bearings —this was anomie, an acute form of alienation that could lead to suicide or aimless riot. By the end of the nineteenth century, alienation came to be used as the term for insanity, derangement of perceived reality; psychiatrists were called alienists.

Contemporary conditions of life have certainly deprived people, and especially young people, of a world meaningful for them in which they can act and realize themselves. Many writers and the dissenting students themselves have spelled out what is wrong. In both schools and corporations, people cannot pursue their own interests, use their powers, exercise initiative. Administrators are hypocrites who sell out people for the smooth operation of their systems. The Cold War has grotesquely distorted reasonable social priorities. Perhaps worst, the powers who make the decisions are incompetent to cope with modern times; two-thirds of mankind are starving, and all are in danger of extinction. For the purposes of this book, let me list some other alienating conditions that call for a religious response.

I have mentioned the lapse of faith in science, which has not produced the general happiness that people expected, and now, under the sway of greed and power, has become frightening. Rationality itself is discredited. Certainly one reason for the fad for astrology and Tarot cards is that they are scientifically ridiculous and dreamy. A hundred years ago, among superstitious peasants, Bazaroff, in *Fathers and Sons,* showed that he was a free spirit by scientifically cutting up frogs and being objective.

Every one of these young grew up since Hiroshima. They do not talk about atom bombs, not nearly so much as we who campaigned against the shelters and fallout; but the bombs explode in their dreams, as Otto Butz found in his study of collegians at San Francisco State College; and George Dennison, in *The Lives of Children,* shows that it is the same with small children in the Lower East Side in New York. Again and again, students have told me that they take it for granted they will not survive the next ten years. This is not an attitude with which to prepare for a career or bring up a family.

Whether or not the bombs go off, human beings are evidently useless. The old are shunted out of sight at an increasingly earlier age; the young are kept on ice till an increasingly later age. Small farmers and other technologically unemployed are dispossessed or left to rot. Increasing millions are put away as incompetent or deviant. Racial minorities that cannot shape up are treated as a nuisance. Together, these groups are a large majority of the population. Since labor is not needed, there is vague talk of a future society of "leisure," but I have heard of no plans for a kind of community in which all human beings would be necessary and valued.

The institutions, technology, and communications have infected even the "biological core," so that people's sexuality and other desires are no longer genuine. One cannot trust in their spontaneous choices. Subliminal suggestions have invaded the unconscious, and superficial pleasure is used as a means of social control, as in *Brave New World*. This was powerfully argued by Wilhelm Reich a generation ago, and it is now repeated by Herbert Marcuse. When I pushed the Reichian position in the forties, I was bitterly attacked as a "bedroom revisionist" by C. Wright Mills and the Marxists, but now it has become orthodoxy among the young militants.

A special aspect of biological corruption is the spreading ugliness, filth, and tension of the environment in which the young grow up. If Wordsworth was right in saying that children must grow up in an environment of beauty and simple affections in order to become trusting, open, and magnanimous adults, then the offspring of our cities, suburbs, and complicated homes have been disadvantaged, no matter how much money there is. This lack cannot be remedied by including Art in the curriculum, nor by vest-pocket playgrounds, nor by banning billboards from bigger highways. Cleaning the river might help, but that will be the day.

And another cause of metaphysical confusion is the sheer prevalence of the man-made, with nothing to compare and contrast it with; everything is stamped with social messages. It has always been the case, in the arts and rhetoric, and in technology in general, that the medium is the message—one cannot separate "form" and "content"; but mass communications are uniquely swamping, all goods are styled and packaged commodities, the medium-message is the only experience. Young people brought up among so much artifice dare not trust the evidence of their own senses and craftsmanship unless it is confirmed on the TV screen or by being on the market; but *these* messages, they know, they certainly can't trust.

iii

If we start from the premise that the young are in a religious crisis, that they doubt there is really a nature of things and they are sure there is no world for themselves, many details of their present behavior become clearer.

Alienation is a powerful motivation, of unrest, fantasy, and reckless action. It can lead, we shall see, to religious innovation, new sacraments to give life meaning. But it is a poor basis for politics, including revolutionary politics.

It is said that the young dissidents never offer a constructive program. And apart from the special cases of Czechoslovakia and Poland, where they confront an unusually outdated system, this is largely true. In other countries, most of the issues of protest have been immediate gut issues, and the tactics have been mainly disruptive, without coherent proposals for a better society. Some American militants say they are "building socialism," but when questioned, they seem to have no institutions in mind, only a dissatisfaction with monopoly capitalism.

This has political difficulties. To have no program rules out the politics of rational persuasion, for there is nothing to offer the other citizens, who do not have one's gut complaints, to get them to come along. Instead, one confronts them with "demands," and they are turned off even when they might otherwise be sympathetic. But the confrontation is inept too, for the alienated young cannot take other people seriously, as having needs and interests of their own; a sad instance was the inability of the French youth to communicate with the French working class in 1968. In Gandhian theory, the confronter aims at future community with the confronted; he will not let him continue a course that is bad for *him,* and so he appeals to his deeper reason. But instead of this Satyagraha, soul force, we have seen plenty of hate. The confronted are not taken as human beings, but as pigs or robots. But how can the young think of a future community with the others when they share no present world with them—no professions, jobs, or trust in the others as human beings? Instead, some young radicals seem to entertain the disastrous illusion that other people can be compelled by frightening them. This can lead only to crushing reaction.

The "political" activity makes sense, however, if it is understood not as aimed at reconstruction at all but as a way of desperately affirming that oneself is alive and wants a place in the sun. "The reason to be a revolutionary in our time," said Cohn-Bendit, leader of the French students, "is that it's a better way to live." And young Americans pathetically and truly say that there is no other way to be taken seriously. Then it is not necessary to have a program; the right way is to act, against any vulnerable point and wherever one can rally support. The purpose is not, narrowly, politics, but to have a movement and form a community. Not surprisingly, this is exactly the recipe that Saul Alinsky prescribed to rally outcaste blacks. And if, like colonialized peoples, one has suffered life-long humiliation, Frantz Fanon adds to the prescription the need to be violent, as psychotherapy.

Such conflictful action has indeed caused social changes. In France it was conceded by the government that "nothing would ever be the same." In the United States, apart from the youth action, the changes in social attitude during the last ten years are unthinkable, with regard to war, corporate administration, the police, the blacks. When the actors have been in touch with the underlying causes of things, issues have deepened and the Movement has grown. But for the alienated, unfortunately, action easily slips into activism and conflict that are largely spite and stubbornness. There is excitement and notoriety, much human suffering, with the world no better off. (*New Left Notes* runs a column wryly called, "We Made the News Today, O Boy!") Then instead of deepening awareness and a sharpening political conflict, there occurs the polarization of mere exasperation. Often it seems that the aim is just to have a shambles. Impatiently the activists raise the ante of their tactics beyond what the "issue" warrants, and support melts away. Out on a limb, the leaders become desperate and fanatical, intolerant of criticism, dictatorial. The Movement falls to pieces.

Yet it is noteworthy that when older people, like myself, are critical of wrongheaded activism, we nevertheless almost invariably concede that the young are *morally* justified. For what is the use of patience when meantime millions are being killed and starved, and when bombs and nerve-gas are being stockpiled? Against entrenched power that does these things, it might be better to do something idiotic, and now, than something perhaps more practical in the long run. I don't know which is less demoralizing.

Maybe a deeper truth was revealed in a conversation I had with a young hippie at a college in Massachusetts. He was dressed like an (American) Indian, in fringed buckskin and a headband, with red paint on his face. All his life, he said, he had tried to escape the encompassing evil of our society that was bent on destroying his soul. "But if you're always escaping," I pointed out, "and never attentively study it, how can you make a wise judgment about society or act effectively either to change it or escape it?" "You see, you don't dig!" he cried. "It's just ideas like 'wise' and 'acting effectively' that we can't stand." He was right. He was in the religious dilemma of Faith versus Works. Where I sat, Works had some reality; I had a vocation that justified me; and I even threw some (tiny) weight in the community. But in the reign of the Devil, as he felt it, "We walk by faith and not by sight." (2 *Corinthians*). But he didn't seem to have Faith either.

If we do not understand their alienation, the young seem dishonorably inconsistent in how they take the present world. Hippies attack technology and are scornful of rationality, but they buy up electronic equipment and motorcycles and with them the whole infrastructure. Militants say that civil liberties are bourgeois and they deny them to others, but they clamor in court for their own civil liberties. Those who say that the university is an agent of the powers that be do not mean thereby to assert the ideal role of the university, but to use the university for their own propaganda. Yet if I point out these apparent inconsistencies, it does not arouse shame or guilt. This has puzzled me. But it is simply that they do not recognize that technology, civil law, and the university are human institutions for which they too are responsible. They take them as brute-given, as just what's there, to be manipulated as convenient. But convenient for whom? The trouble with this attitude is that these institutions, works of spirit in history, are how Man has made himself and is. If they treat them as mere things and are not vigilant for them, do not they themselves become very little?

Their lack of sense of history is bewildering. It is impossible to convey to them that the deeds of the past were done by human beings, that John Hamden committed civil disobedience and refused the war tax just as we do, or that Beethoven, just like a rock and roll band, made up his music as he went along, from odds and ends, with energy, spontaneity, and passion—how else do they think he made music?

They no longer remember their own history. A few years ago there was a commonly accepted story of mankind. Mankind (var. *Californiensis*) sprang into existence, from nothing, with the Beats, went on to the Chessman case, the HUAC bust, and the Freedom rides; and came to maturity with the Berkeley Victory, "the first human event in forty thousand years," as Mike Rossman told me. But this year I find that nothing antedates Chicago '68. Each coming class is more entangled in the specious present. Elder statesmen like Sidney Lens and Staughton Lynd have been trying with heroic effort to recall the American antecedents of radical and libertarian slogans and tactics, but it doesn't rub off. I am often hectored to my face with formulations that I myself put in their mouths, which have become part of oral tradition two years old, author prehistoric. Most significant of all, it has been whispered to me—but I can't check up because I don't speak the language—that in junior high, for ages thirteen and fourteen, that's really where it's at! Quite different from what goes on in the colleges that I visit.

What I do see is that dozens of Underground newspapers have the same noisy style and stereotyped content: "A brother throws a canister at a pig." Though each one is doing his thing, there is not much idiosyncrasy in so much spontaneous variety. As if mesmerized, the political radicals repeat the power plays, factionalism, random abuse, and tactical lies that aborted the movement in the thirties. And I have learned, to my disgust, that the reason why young people don't trust people over thirty is that they don't understand them and are afraid to try. Having grown up in a world too meaningless to them for them to learn anything, they know very little and are quick to resent it. Their resentment is understandable; what is disgusting is their lack of moral courage.

Needless to say, the atmosphere is rife with paranoia. The hostile inexperience of the young, with a chip on the shoulder and fortified by ideology, calls out to the latent lunacy of the reactionaries; and the dream world perforce becomes the public world, because they are all our fellow citizens. There will be a couple of massacres before, hopefully, there is a revulsion of common sense. Last month—I am writing in June 1969—a police helicopter gassed the campus of the University of California. The reason for this was that some enterprising hippies were developing a vacant lot of the university as a garden with swings, but the chancellor's office had decided it must be developed as a soccer field.*

i v

This is not a pleasant account. Even so, the alienated *have* no vital alternative except to confront the Enemy, and to try to make a new way of life out of their own innards. As they are doing.

It is irrelevant to show that the System is not the monolith that they think and that most people are not very corrupt but just confused and anxious. The point is that they cannot see this, because they do not have a world operable for them. In such a case, the only advice that I would dare to give is that which Krishna gave Arjuna: to confront with non-attachment, to be brave and firm without hatred. (I don't want to discuss here the question of violence; the disdain and hatred are more important.) Also, when they

* My guess is that in the School of Architecture of the university, the do-it-yourself method of the hippies in this case is being taught as a model of correct urban landscape architecture, to encourage citizenship and eliminate vandalism, according to the ideas of Karl Linn and others. The chancellor could just as well have given out academic credit and an A grade.

are seeking a new way of life, I find that I urge them occasionally to write a letter home.

As a citizen and father, I have a right to try to prevent a shambles and to diminish the number of wrecked lives. But it is improper for older people to keep saying, as we do, that activity of the young is "counterproductive." It's our business to do something more productive that they can join if they want to.

Religiously the young have been inventive, much more than the God-is-dead theologians. They have hit on new sacraments, physical actions to get them out of their estrangement and break through (momentarily) into meaning. The terribly loud music is used sacramentally—which, incidentally, should be taken into account by those who say it is bad for the hearing; they are welded together in the block of clamor. The claim for the hallucinogenic drugs is almost never the nirvana of opium nor the escape from distress of heroin, but tuning in to the cosmos and communing with one another. They seem to have had flashes of success in bringing ritual participation back into theater, which for a hundred years playwrights and directors have tried to do in vain. And whatever the political purposes and political results of activism, there is no doubt that shared danger for righteousness' sake is used sacramentally as baptism of fire. Fearful moments of provocation and the poignant release of the bust bring unconscious contents to the surface, create a bond of solidarity, are "commitment."

The most powerful magic, working in all these sacraments, is the close presence of other human beings, without competition or one-upping. The original sin is to be on an ego trip. Angry political factionalism has now also become a bad thing. It is a drastic comment on the dehumanization and fragmentation of modern times that salvation can be attained simply by the "warmth of assembled animal bodies," as Kafka called it, describing his Mice. At the 1967 Easter Be-In in Central Park in New York, when about ten thousand were crowded on the Sheep Meadow, a young man with a quite radiant face said to me, "Gee, human beings are legal!"—it was sufficient to be exempted from harassment by bureaucratic rules and officious police. A small group passing a joint of marijuana often behaves like a Quaker meeting waiting for the spirit, and the cigarette may be a placebo. T-groups and sensitivity training, with Mecca at Esalen, have the same idea. And I think this is the sense of the sexuality, which is certainly not hedonistic, nor mystical in the genre of D. H. Lawrence, nor does it have much to do with personal love, which is too threatening for these anxious youths. But it is human touch, without conquest or domination, and it obviates self-consciousness and embarrassed speech.

A hippie who had helped construct the People's Park in Berkeley said that it was the first time in his life that he had ever enjoyed working hard, because it was "their own." One realizes with dismay that he had probably never repaired his bike as his own, nor painted the house as his own family's, nor studied a subject because it was interesting to himself, nor cooperated with his friends on an enterprise simply because they thought it worthwhile. Everything was sequestered as Papa's or as part of the curriculum or part of the System. It was necessary to live through alienation and confrontation in order to feel something was "one's own." It was necessary to do it in a gang in order to be oneself.

Around this pure but difficult faith, so dependent on its adversaries, and on confused allies, there has collected a mess of eclectic and exotic liturgy and paraphernalia, for there is no natural or primitive traditional expression: mandalas, beggars in saffron (not quite the right shade), (American) Indian beads, lectures on Zen. The exotic is desirable because it is not what they have grown up with. And it is true that fundamental facts of life are more acceptable if they come in fancy dress; for instance, it is good to breathe from the diaphragm and one can learn to do this by humming OM, especially in anxious conditions, as Allen Ginsberg did for seven hours in Jackson Park in Chicago. But college chaplains of the usual faiths are also pretty busy, and they are now more likely to see the adventurous and offbeat than, as used to be the case, the staid and square. Flowers and the poems of Blake have a certain authenticity of tradition, in the line of the English Romantics and the Angel Pre-Raphael. The "psychedelic" biomorphic drawing that decorates the Underground papers is poor, but it carries on the urge to naturalness of William Morris and the decaying flora and fauna of Aubrey Beardsley and Art Nouveau. Conversely, although the almost ubiquitous guitars and mountain harmony are phony—in fact, they were co-opted by the Stalinists in the thirties as a ploy of the Popular Front—the electrifying of the instruments is indigenous and the deafening noise is authentically pathetic. So are the strobe lights and the immersion in technologically controlled spaces.

It is hard to describe this, or any, religiosity without lapsing into condescending humor. Yet it is genuine and it will, I am convinced, survive and develop, I don't know into what. In the end, it is religion that constitutes the strength of the new generation. It is not, as I used to think, their morality, political will, or frank common sense. Except for a few, I am not impressed by their moral courage or even honesty. For all their eccentricity, they are quite lacking in personality. They do not have enough world to have strong character. They are not especially attractive (to me) as animals. But they keep pouring out a kind of metaphysical vitality.

There is a natural cause for religion: impasse. On the one hand, these young have an unusual amount of available psychic energy from childhood. They were brought up on antibiotics that minimized depressing chronic childhood diseases. They had the post-Freudian freedom to act out their early drives and not develop exhausting inhibitions. Up to age six or seven, television nourished them with masses of strange images and sometimes true information; McLuhan makes a lot of sense for the kindergarten years (it is only later that TV diminishes experience). Long schooling would tend to make them stupid, but it has been compensated by providing the vast isolated cities of youth that the high schools and colleges essentially are, where they can incubate their own thoughts. They are sexually precocious and superficially knowledgeable. Nevertheless, all this available psychic energy has had little practical use. The social environment is dehumanized. They cannot use their own initiative. They are desperately bored because the world does not promise any fulfillment—it is the promise, however far-fetched, of fulfillment that makes it possible to be in love. Their kind of knowledge gives no intellectual or poetic satisfaction; it mostly makes them kibitzers.

In this impasse, we can expect a ferment of new religion. As in Greek plays, impasse produces gods from the machine. For a long time we did not hear of the symptoms of adolescent religious conversion, once as common in the United States as in all other places and ages. Now it is recurring as a mass phenomenon.

V

There is no doubt that the religious young are in touch with something historical, but I don't think that they understand what it is. Let me quote from the *New Seminary News*, the newsletter of dissident seminarians from the Pacific School of Religion in Berkeley: "What we confront —willingly or not we are thrust into it—is a time of disintegration of a dying civilization and the emergence of a new one." This seems to envisage something like the instant decline of the Roman Empire, and they, presumably, are like the primitive Christians about to build, out of their hats, another era.

But there are no signs that this is the actual situation. It would mean, for instance, that our scientific technology, civil law, professions, universities, communications, etc., etc., are about to vanish from the earth to be replaced by something entirely different. This is a fantasy of alienated minds. The proposition of the New Seminarians is apocalyptic—the content is St. Mark or St. Paul—but the style and format are conventional. Nobody behaves as if civilization would vanish, and nobody acts as if there were a new dispensation and a new heaven and earth with pneumatic laws. Nobody is waiting patiently in the catacombs and the faithful have not withdrawn into the desert. Neither the Yippies nor the New Seminarians nor any other exalted group have produced anything that is the least bit miraculous. The Yippies promised to levitate the Pentagon, but it did not rise. In A.D. 300 it would have risen six feet while four angels stood at the corners of the world and blew horns; a hundred thousand people would have testified to it. Our civilization may well destroy itself with atom bombs or something else, but then we do not care what will emerge, if anything.

But the actual situation, I have been arguing, *is* very like 1510, when Luther went to Rome, the eve of the Reformation. Everywhere there is protest, conflict, disgust with the Establishment. The protest is international. There is a generation gap. We must recall that Luther himself was all of thirty when he posted the Theses in 1517. Melanchthon was twenty, Bucer twenty-six, Münzer twenty-eight, Jonas twenty-four. The Movement consisted of undergraduates and junior faculty.

The main thrust of protest has not been to give up science, technology, and civil institutions, but to purge them, humanize them, decentralize them, change the priorities, stop the drain of wealth. These were the demands of the March 4th teach-in of the dissenting scientists. That event and the waves of other teach-ins, ads, and demonstrations have been the voices not of alienation, of people who have no world, but of protestantism, people deep in the world who will soon refuse to continue under the present auspices because they are not viable. It is a populism permeated by moral and professional unease. What the young have done is to bring on a religious crisis to make it impossible to continue in such moral unease.

The milieu in which the protest first broke out has been, inevitably, the overgrown monkish school systems. But it is not yet clear to either the protesting students or professors that the essential target of protest is these otiose institutions themselves. In my opinion, much of the student little to do with the excellent political and social demands that are made, but is the result of boredom and resentment dissent in the colleges and especially the high schools has because of the phoniness of the whole academic enterprise. I shall return to this in Chapter 5.

Viewed as incidents of a Reformation, as attempts of the alienated young to purge themselves and recover lost integrity, the various movements are easily recognizable as characteristic protestant sects, intensely self-conscious. The dissenting seminarians of the Pacific School of Religion or of the Jewish Theological Seminary in New York do not intend to go off to primitive love feasts or back to Father Abraham, but to form their own free seminary; that is, they are Congregationalists. Shaggy hippies are not nature children, as they claim, but self-conscious Adamites trying to naturalize Sausalito and the East Village. Heads are Pentecostals. Those who spindle IBM cards and throw the dean downstairs are Iconoclasts. The critique of the Organization is strongly Jansenist. Those who want a say in the rules and curriculum mean to deny Infant Baptism, like Petrobrusians. Radicals who live among the poor and try to politicize them are certainly intent on social change, but they are also trying to find themselves again, like the young nobles of the Waldenses and Lollards. The support of the black revolt is desperately like Anabaptism, but God grant that we can do better than the Peasants' War. The statement of Cohn-Bendit that I quoted before, that the reason to be a revolutionary is that it is the best way of life at present, is unthinkable from either a political revolutionary or a man imbued with primitive religious faith, but it is hard-core self-conscious protestantism.

These analogies are not fanciful. When authority is discredited, there is a pattern in the return of the repressed. A better scholar could make a longer list; but the reason I here spell it out is that, perhaps, some young person will suddenly remember that history was about something.

Naturally, traditional churches are themselves in transition. On college campuses and in bohemian neighborhoods, existentialist Protestants and Jews and updating Catholics have taken a place in political and social conflict and, what is more important, they have changed their own moral, esthetic, and personal tone. With excruciating slowness, in a dehumanized society, they are recollecting that religion has some essential relation to human beings, and humanity is in danger. Yet it seems to me that, in their new zeal for relevance, chaplains are badly failing in their chief duty to the religious young, which is to be professors of theology. Because of the generation gap, they certainly cannot perform pastoral services like advice or consolation, which the young insist on doing for themselves. Chaplains say that the young are uninterested in dogma and are intractable on this level, but I think this is simply a projection of their own distaste for the conventional theology that has gone dead for them. The young are hotly metaphysical, but alas, boringly so, because they think the world began yesterday; they have no language to express their intuitions, and they repeat every old fallacy. If the chaplains would stop looking in the conventional places where God is dead, and would explore the actualities where perhaps He is alive, they might learn something and have something to teach.

PART TWO

Education
of the Young

Chapter 5

i

In advanced countries, a chief cause—perhaps the chief cause—of alienation of the young has been the school systems themselves. It is ironical. The purpose of education is to help each youngster find his calling, the work in the community that fulfills him and, as Luther said, justifies him; yet we go to extraordinary effort and expense to provide schools that estrange him, that convince him that he has no calling and no adult community, and that nobody pays attention to him.

Many explanations are given for the rebellion in the colleges and high schools—the students demand Student Power, blacks want community control, and administrators say they need more money; but nobody wants to suggest that maybe so much schooling for so many is not a good idea. In my opinion, the majority of so-called students in college and high schools do not want to be there and ought not to be. An academic environment is not the appropriate means of education for most young people, including most of the bright.

The present expanded school systems are coercive in their nature. The young have to attend for various well-known reasons, none of which is necessary for their well-being or the well-being of society. Then when a small militant group defies the coercive institution and shouts "Shut it down!"—the leader of the student uprising at Columbia in 1968 said, "I hate Columbia"—the majority are coolly complacent because they don't care for the place either. And since the catch-all expansion makes serious academic work impossible, many of the faculty are complacent about the shut-down too. If the police move in brutally, as has commonly happened, there is a surging of youth loyalty and faculty fatherliness, which are authentic, unlike the school itself. For a spell, the small minority leads the majority.

In brief, every one of these campus disorders is essentially a prison riot. If the schools were truly voluntary associations, the disorders would never occur or would be immediately quelled by the members who would protect what they love.

As it is, it looks as if the course of events will be as follows. The disorders will increase. A certain number of schools, especially high schools—and perhaps in rich suburban neighborhoods—will be burned down. It seems likely that in the next few years the children in junior high school are going to play truant in droves. Taxpayers will finally refuse to pay for this kind of thing; in 1969 new school bond proposals are already being voted down. Adolescents will then be out on the streets with no provision for their education at all. In this emergency, some other people will begin to say what I am saying now.

ii

To be educated well or badly, to learn by a long process to cope with the physical environment and the culture of one's society, is part of the human condition; and in every society the education of the children is of the highest importance. But in all societies, both primitive and highly civilized, until quite recently most education of most children has occurred incidentally, not in schools set aside for the purpose. Adults did their economic work and other social tasks; children were not excluded, were paid attention to, and learned to be included. The children were not formally "taught." In many adult institutions, incidental education has always been taken for granted as an essential part of the functioning, e.g. in families and age peer groups, community labor, master-apprentice arrangements, games and plays, prostitution and other sexual initiation, and religious rites. In Greek *paideia,* the entire network of institutions, the *polis,* was thought of as an educator. As John Dewey beautifully put it, the essence of all philosophy is the philosophy of education, the study of how to have a world.

By and large, though not for all topics and all persons, the incidental process of education suits the nature of learning better than formal teaching. The young see real causes and effects rather than pedagogic exercises. Reality is often complex, but the young incidental learner, of whom not too much is expected, can take it by his own handle, at his own time, according to his own interest and initiative. And he can imitate, identify, be approved or disapproved, cooperate and compete, without the embarrassment and sometimes chilling anxiety of being the center of attention and demand. So there is socialization with less resentment, fear, or submission. The archetype of successful education is infants learning to speak, a formidable intellectual achievement that is universally accomplished. We do not know how it is done, but the main conditions seem to be the incidental process we have been describing. (I discuss this in the next chapter.)

Along with incidental education, however, most societies also have institutions specifically devoted to teaching the young. Such are identity rites, catechism, nurses and pedagogues, youth houses, formal schooling. I think there is usually a peculiar aspect to what is learned by such means rather than picked up incidentally, and we must ask further about this. But let me emphasize strongly and repeatedly that it is only in the last century in industrialized countries that the majority of children have gotten much formal teaching at all, and it is only in the past few decades that formal schooling has been massively extended into adolescence and further. In the United States in 1900 only 6 percent went through high school and ¼ percent through college. Yet now, formal schooling has taken over, well or badly, very much of the more natural incidental education of most other institutions.

This may or may not be necessary, but it has consequences. The other institutions, and the adults in them, have correspondingly lost touch with the young, and the young do not know the adults in their chief activities. We saw in the last chapter, for instance, how the professions have vanished from reality for the young, even though academic schooling is aimed toward the professions. Like the jails and insane asylums, schools isolate society from its problems, whether preventing crime, curing mental disease, or bringing up the young. And conversely, to a remarkable degree, vital functions of growing up have become hermetically redefined in school terms: being a good citizen is doing homework; apprenticeship is passing tests for jobs in the distant future; sexual initiation is high school dating; rites of passage are getting diplomas. Crime is breaking school windows, and rebellion is sitting in on the dean. In the absence of adult culture, there develops a youth subculture.

Usually there has been a rough distinction in content, in what is learned, between incidental education and intentional pedagogy. Social business that does not exclude children tends to be matter-of-fact, and children, taking part without anxiety, can be objective about it, if not critical. But intentional pedagogy, whether directed by elders, priests, or academics, has to do with what is not evident in ordinary affairs; it teaches what is more scholarly, abstract, intangible, or mysterious, and the learner, as the center of attention and demand, is under personal pressure. All social activity socializes its participants, but pedagogy socializes deliberately, according to principles; it has stricter standards, often tested and graded, instilling the morals and habits which are the social bonds.

There are, of course, two opposite interpretations of why pedagogues want to indoctrinate, and in my opinion both are correct. On the one hand, the elders, priests, and schoolteachers are instilling an ideology to support their own system of control and exploitation, including the domination of the old over the young, and they have to make a special effort to awe, confuse, and mystify because the system does not recommend itself to common sense. At present, when formal education swallows up so much young life and pretends to be practical preparation for every activity and every walk of life, ideological processing is deadly. Those who succumb to it have no wits of their own left.

On the other hand, there perhaps *is* important information, abstract or vague, that must be passed on but that does not appear on the surface on ordinary occasions and that requires personal instruction, special pointing out, repetition, cloistered reflection. Thus, it is now the popular wisdom that we cannot work a high technology without great amounts of book-learning for every child and adolescent. And interestingly enough, dissenting students, who have no interest in this technical or professional learning, nevertheless complain that professors do not give them personal attention. Apparently they believe that there is some wisdom to be picked up in an academic setting. But God forbid that you offer it.

Champions of liberal arts colleges say that training for the high technology is not a big deal, since one way or another the young will pick up contemporary know-how and mores without colleges; but the greatness of mankind—Hippocrates and Beethoven, the Enlightenment, civil liberties, the sense of the tragic—will lapse without a trace unless the scholars work at transmitting it. I sympathize with this problem as they state it, and I will return to it, but in fact I have not heard of any method whatever, scholastic or otherwise, to *teach* the humanities without killing them. Myself, I remember how at age twelve, while browsing in the library, I read *Macbeth* with excitement, but in class I could not understand a word of *Julius Caesar* and hated it; and I think this has been the usual experience of people who read and write well. The survival of the humanities has seemed to depend on random miracles, which are becoming less frequent.

Finally, unlike incidental learning which is natural and inevitable, formal schooling is a deliberate intervention and must justify itself. We must ask not only is it well done and how to do it better, but is it worth doing and *can* it be well done? Is direct teaching possible at all? There is a line of critics from Lao-tse and Socrates to Carl Rogers who assert that there is no such thing as teaching of either science or virtue; and there is strong empirical evidence that schooling has little effect on either vocational ability or citizenship. Donald Hoyt, for American College Testing, 1965, found that college grades have no correlation with life achievement in any profession; David Cohen, for the New York Board of Regents, reviewing all the evidence since 1925, found that there was little correlation between what the high schools have pretended to and what they have accomplished.

At the other extreme, Dr. Skinner and the operant-conditioners claim that they can "instruct" for every kind of performance, they can control and shape human behavior as they can with animals; and this includes sophisticated intellectual activity like reasoning (compare Loren Resnick, *Harvard Educational Review*, Fall 1963), though they are careful to say that they do not educate in the sense of "developing persons," whatever that might mean. (Since operant-conditioning requires the sealing off of the animals from the ordinary environment, however, it is disputable whether human children are good subjects for this kind of instruction in any society we like to envisage.)

In the middle, the main line of educators, from Confucius and Aristotle to John Dewey, hold that, starting from the natural motives of the young, one can teach them good habits of morals, arts, and sciences by practice, including academic exercises. Self-motivated, the learners take on a "second nature" which they can then further apply by themselves. And on various theories, Froebel, Herbart, Steiner, or Piaget have held that such teaching is possible if it addresses the child's growing powers in the right order at the right moments.

On the other hand, sociologists like Comte or Marx seem to say that the background social institutions and their vicissitudes overwhelmingly determine what is learned, so that it is not worthwhile to discuss pedagogy, at least as yet. And the influence of the peer group certainly seems to outweigh the formal efforts of schoolteachers.

I will not pursue this topic here, but we should bear in mind that such fundamental disagreements exist. My bias is that "teaching" is largely a delusion. People do learn by practice, but not much by academic exercises in an academic setting.

i i i

Turn now to actual formal schooling in the United States, the country most technologically advanced, but the story is not much different in other developed and developing countries, including China and Cuba. The school system, expanding and increasingly tightly integrated, has taken over a vast part of the educational functions of society, designing preschool toys from age two, and training for every occupation as well as citizenship, sexuality, and the humanities. Yet with trivial exceptions, what we mean by school—namely a special place with a curriculum generalized from the activities of life, divided into departments, using texts, lessons, scheduled periods marked by bells, specialist teachers, examinations, and graded promotion to the next step up the ladder—is a sociological invention of some Irish monks in the seventh century to bring a bit of Rome to wild shepherds. It is an amazing success story, probably more important than the Industrial Revolution.

At first, no doubt, it was a good thing for wild shepherds to have to sit still for a couple of hours and pay strict attention to a foreign language, penmanship, and spelling. The total strangeness of what they learned made the halting deliberate academic process the only one possible, as one learns nonsense syllables by small doses and review. And mostly it was only aspiring clerics who were schooled. By a historical accident, the same academic method later became the way of teaching the bookish part of a couple of other learned professions, law and medicine. There is no essential reason why law and medicine are not better learned by apprenticeship in real practice, but the bookish was clerical and therefore scholastic, and (I guess) any special education containing abstract principles was part of the system of mysteries, therefore clerical, and therefore scholastic.

This monkish rule of scheduled hours, texts, and lessons is also not an implausible method for giving a quick background briefing to large numbers, who then embark on their real business—and real education. Thus Jefferson insisted on universal compulsory schooling, for short terms, in predominantly rural communities, so children could read the newspapers and be catechized in libertarian political history in order to become citizens in a Jeffersonian democracy. Later, in compulsory urban schools, the children of polyglot immigrants were socialized and taught standard English, a peculiar dialect, so they could then try to make good in an economy which needed them and indeed proved to be fairly open to their advancement in the long run. The curriculum was the English penmanship, spelling, and arithmetic useful for the business world. Naturally, the forced socialization involved drastic cultural disruption and family fragmentation, but perhaps it was not a bad solution —we really have yet to see how it works out.

At present, however, the context of compulsory schooling is entirely different. The monkish invention is now used as universal social engineering. Society is conceived as a controlled system of personnel and transactions—with various national goals, depending on the nation—and the schools are the teaching machine for all personnel. There is no other way of entry for the young. And teaching tries to give not only a few background skills but technical and psychological preparation in depth. Schooling for one's role, in graded steps, takes up to twenty years and more, and is the chief activity of growing up. Any other interest may be interrupted for school-going and homework. The real motivation for a five-year-old's behavior, therefore, is geared to the future, fifteen years hence; and there is thus an inevitable problem of motivating *him* to behave the behavior.

In technologies with a high productivity like ours, of course, where manpower is not needed, a more realistic interpretation is that the social function of long schooling is to keep the useless and obstreperous young *away* from the delicate social machine, to baby-sit and police them. Yet the exclusion comes to the same thing as processing. The schools are not run like playgrounds or reservations, but as institutions for training. Whether by accident or design, the texture of school experience is similar to that of adult experience. There is little break between playing with educational toys and watching ETV, being in grade school and the Little League, being in high school and dating, being in college and being drafted, being personnel of a corporation and watching NBC. It is a curious historical question whether the schools have been transformed on the model of business organization or the adult world has become scholastic. The evidence is that, up to about 1920, business methods had a preponderant influence (compare the excellent study by Daniel Callahan, *The Cult of Efficiency in American Education*). But especially since 1945 and the expansion of university-based research and development, the school monks have increasingly determined the social style, and adults have become quite puerile. It is astounding to hear grown men of the middle class say how much better informed their children are than themselves, meaning they are more verbal in a schoolboyish way.

Since the trend has been to eliminate incidental education and prepare the young formally for every aspect of ordinary life, we would expect pedagogy to become secularized and functional, e.g., for machinery to be taught by mechanics. But the reverse has been the case. Schooling has not only remained scholastic, but is increasingly suffused with ritual and social control. Radical students complain that the schooling is ideological and "irrelevant" (= abstract) through and through. The simplest, and not altogether superficial, explanation of the paradox is that scholastic mystery has transformed ordinary adult business. Society is run by mandarins, the New Class.

Even on its own terms, this is not working well. Schooling costs more than armaments, but it does not in fact prepare for jobs and professions. I have referred to the studies to this effect of Donald Hoyt and David Cohen. Evidence compiled by Ivar Berg of Columbia shows (in *New Generation*, Winter 1968) that dropouts do as well as high school graduates in less pretentious jobs. The schools do not provide peaceful baby-sitting and policing. Instead of being an efficient teaching machine, gearing the young to the rest of the social machine, the schools seem to run for their own sakes, accumulating bluebooks. There is a generation gap. Many of the young fail or drop out. Others picket or riot. Predictably, the response of school administrators is to refine the processing, to make the curriculum still more relevant, to enrich the curriculum, to add remedial steps, to study developmental psychology for new points of manipulation, to start earlier, to use new teaching technology, to eliminate friction by admitting students to administrative positions.

Let me propose, rather, that social engineering, and any teaching machine, are uneducational in principle. They try, according to somebody else's ideas, to prestructure a kind of behavior, learning, that can be discriminating, graceful, and energetic only if the organism itself creates its own structures as it goes along. Schooling inefficiently rules out too many human powers to learn.

In the long run, human powers are the chief resources. In the short run, unused powers assert themselves anyway and make trouble. And cramped powers produce distorted or labile effects. If we set up a structure that strictly channels energy, directs attention, and regulates movement (which, to pedagogues, are "good things"), we may temporarily inhibit impulse, wishing, daydreaming, and randomness (which are "bad things"), but we also thereby jeopardize initiative, intrinsic motivation, imagination, invention, self-reliance, freedom from inhibition, and finally even common sense and health. Except in emergencies or special cases, this is likely to be fatally wasteful. It is frequently said that human beings use only a small part—2 percent—of their abilities, so some educators propose much more demanding and intellectual tasks at a much earlier age. And there is no doubt that most children can think and learn far more than they are challenged to. Yet it is likely that by far the greatest waste of ability, including intellectual and creative ability, occurs because a playful, hunting, sexy, dreamy, combative, passionate, artistic, manipulative and destructive, jealous and magnanimous, and selfish and disinterested animal is continually thwarted by social organization and perhaps especially by schooling. If so, the main reform of pedagogy at present is to counteract and delay socialization as long as possible (and I shall suggest a method for this in Chapter 6). Our situation is the opposite of the seventh century: Since the world has become scholastic, we must protect the wild shepherds.

The personal attitude of schoolteachers toward the young is problematic. I can understand that adults are protective and helpful to small children, and that professionals in graduate schools want apprentices to carry on; but why would grownups spend whole days hanging around adolescents and callow collegians? They are sexually interesting and this must be a common motive, but it is strongly disapproved and its inhibition makes for a bad situation. Traditional motives have been to domineer and be a big fish in a small pond. The present preferred posture seems to me to be extremely dishonest. It is to take a warm interest in the young as persons while getting them to perform according to an impersonal schedule. Since from the teacher's, or supervisor's, point of view the performance is the essence, if a student fails, the interest can quickly degenerate into being harsh for the student's own good or hating him as an incorrigible animal. I do not see any functional way to recruit a large corps of high school teachers. With incidental education there is no problem. Most people like the young to be around and to watch them develop, and their presence often makes a job more honest and less routine, for they are honest and not routine.

Put this another way: The vagaries of small children do not threaten most normal adults, except parents; one can tolerate them, cope with them, and perhaps turn them to the child's advantage. But the vagaries of teen-agers and collegians are threatening to most adults, and must be put down or co-opted, unless the grownup is unusually sage. The only authentic way of withstanding youthful pressure is to affirm one's own beliefs and go about one's own business, and then the young must cope if they want to take part. This again makes for incidental education, but it is not "teaching."

iv

Current high thought among schoolmen—for instance, at the National Science Foundation and the Harvard School of Education—is to criticize the syllabus as indeed wasteful and depressing, but to urge still more schooling and make the instruction more psychological. Rote learning and teaching of "facts" are disesteemed, though these were at least something that schools could do, such as it was. Rather, since the frontier of knowledge is changing so rapidly, it is said, there is no use in burdening children with knowledge that will be outdated in ten years, and with skills that will soon be better performed by ubiquitous machines.

The formula is that children must learn to learn; their cognitive faculties must be developed; they should be taught the Big Ideas, like Evolution or the Conservation of Energy. (This is what Robert Hutchins was saying forty years ago.) Or it is proposed that children must not be "taught" but allowed to discover for themselves; they must be encouraged to guess and brainstorm rather than be tested on the right answers.

In my opinion, in an academic setting these proposals are never bona fide. As Gregory Bateson has noticed with dolphins and trainers and as John Holt has noticed in middle class schools, learning to learn usually means picking up the structure of behavior of the teachers and becoming expert in the academic process. In actual practice, young discoverers are bound to discover what will get them past the College Board examinations. Guessers and dreamers are not really free to balk and drop out for a semester to brood and let their theories germinate in the dark, as proper geniuses do. And what if precisely the Big Ideas are not true? Einstein said that it was preferable to have a stupid pedant for a teacher so that a smart child could fight him all the way and develop his own thought.

It is a crucial question whether "cognitive faculties" does not mean the syntax of school performance. There is an eccentric passage in an early work of Piaget where he says that children in the playground seem to be using intellectual concepts, e.g. causality, a couple of years earlier than they are "developed" in the classroom; but he sticks to the classroom situation because it allows for his scientific observation. Yet if this is so, it might mean either or both of two things: that the formal routine of the classroom has hindered the spontaneous use of the intellect; or even worse, that the "concept" which is developed in the classroom is in part not intellectual at all but is a method of adjustment to the classroom, the constricted seats, the schedule, the teacher's expectation, the inherently not very interesting subject matter to which one must pay attention anyway. Then "cognitive development" would mean learning the school ropes and becoming life-stupider.

I think the pedagogic reasoning of Harvard and the National Science Foundation is something like this: There is a function and style of science which they, as scientists, know; and there must be some more efficient way to give the young the tools and language of it than to teach them to painfully learn the habit of science by doing science. This pre-training is now necessary because of the complicated technological environment and the complexity of modern science; and there is little room in streamlined Big Science for beginners. If they are not licked into shape, how will the young cope? This is certainly an earnest concern, and I certainly do not know the answer.

Yet I think it is a mistake to look for a scholastic solution. This was the mistake of Dewey's earlier attempt to domesticate industrialism by "learning by doing" *in school*. In the first place, we older people must notice that the technological environment is not nearly so arcane to the young as it is to us. Since it *is* the environment, its ideas permeate the culture. Let me give a striking example. Three of my hippie friends, inveterate dropouts, can design computer circuits, which equally intelligent people of my generation, including myself, cannot do at all. One learned it in the Army, another in an insane asylum, another just picked it up. What *would* the young experience and learn except what is important in the environment? A child who can't count can always make change for a dollar. There is a poignant dilemma specific to a schoolteacher: something is evident to a child, but in order to make it clear to himself so that he can teach it the teacher makes it incomprehensible to the child.

I agree that new times and new topics require new symbols, and they may even, though I am not convinced of this, require new patterns of thinking. But schoolteachers decide that these must be taught in graded steps from *the* elements that they themselves were brought up on, and theorists of cognition exhibit the same wooden attitude in adding new levels of abstraction. (Sometimes there is a flurry of simplification like New Math.) But experience determines its own elements. To those brought up on them, new times are not new, they are just the times. And in my opinion, Prince Kropotkin beautifully solved the cognitive problem of levels of abstraction when he said, you can explain any scientific proposition to an unlettered peasant if you yourself understand it concretely. For then you know, from your shared experience, by what handle to take it; you can appreciate his way of taking it. And if you don't understand it concretely, as making a difference in your own life, are you sure it's relevant to teach?

Let me put it another way. Two hundred years ago, Immanuel Kant exhaustively and accurately mapped the territory that our new cognitive theorists are exploring in fragments and with occasional blunders.* Kant showed that

---

* For example, consider the following statement of J. S. Bruner of Harvard: "We organize experience to represent not only the particulars that have been experienced, but the classes of events of which the particulars are exemplars. We go not only from part to whole, but irresistibly from the particular to the general." I should think, rather, that we organize experience as a major part of the experience itself, and not to represent anything; a gestalt is not a symbol. By and large we start from the confused general or global and specify it; as Aristotle said, a baby first calls every man Daddy and then distinguishes Tom and Dick. And no animal normally goes from part to whole unless totally baffled by mazes, obsessional neurosis, or schoolteachers. For instance, the normal Rorschach response is to large areas or wholes, not to details. What Bruner means to say, I think, is that to program a computer according to current symbolic logic, which is extensional, we organize "experience" in this way. But this is rather a specialized

our intellectual structures come into play spontaneously, by the "synthetic unity of apperception," if we are attentive in real situations. They certainly seem to do so when infants learn to speak. The problem of knowing is to have attentive experience, to get people to pay attention, without cramping the unifying play of free intellectual powers. Schools are bad at this. Interesting reality is good. On the other hand, according to Kant, to exercise the cognitive faculties abstractly, *ante rem*, in themselves, is precisely superstition, presumptuous theology. He wrote all this in *The Critique of Pure Reason*, which I would strongly recommend to the Harvard School of Education. In another work, on child care, he said, "We must allow children freedom so they may learn to use their powers"—he was advising against using swaddling clothes.

V

Progressive education is best defined as a reaction to schooling that has become cramping; its purpose is to liberate what has been distorted or repressed in children growing up.

Progressive education is always a political movement, for the exclusion of a human power or style of life is the effect of a social injustice, and progressive education emerges when the social problem is breaking out. To say this more positively, an old regime, with its method of schooling, is not adequate to new conditions; new energy and new character are needed in order to cope. What the progressive educator thinks of as the "nature" of the child, which he is trying to conserve and nourish, is what he intuits will work best in the world. The form that progressive education takes in each era is prophetic of the next social revolution. Thus, a rosy history of progressive education might look like this:

---

function to saddle all children with, most of whose logic is, hopefully, intensional.

Rousseau was reacting to the artificiality and in-sincerity of the court, the parasitism of the courtiers, the formality, and the pervasive superstition. Apart from its moral defects, such a regime had become simply incompetent to govern, and a generation later it indeed abdicated. Because of the foreign invasions and the Terror, the French Revolution did not fulfill itself morally, but Rousseau's vision was really achieved in the first decades of the American republic, where the ideal of education and character—to be frank and unadorned, empirical, self-reliant, proudly independent—could have been drawn from *Émile*, as *Émile* itself had been drawn from the Americans.

John Dewey was reacting to the genteel culture irrelevant to industrial society, rococo decoration, puritanism that denied animal nature, self-censored literature, robber-baron individualism, rote perform-ance in school and factory. And again, after a genera-tion, by the end of the New Deal, this moral vision had largely come to be. Most of the program of Populism and the labor movement was law; education and cul-ture (among whites) had become utilitarian and fairly classless; the revolution of Freud and Spock was well advanced; architecture and design had become func-tionalist; and there was all manner of social organiza-tion and togetherness rather than individualism.

A. S. Neill's Summerhill, our recent style of pro-gressive education, has been a reaction to social engi-neering, the trend to 1984; which meant obedience to organizational rules, role-playing instead of being, destruction of community by meritocracy, objective knowledge without personal commitment. Since, for children, getting to class is the immutable nature of things, Neill transformed reality when he made this a matter of choice. When he gave to small children authentic self-government and power, he challenged the charisma of all authoritarian institutions. And again progressive education has been prescient. The evidence is that we may yet have a universal shambles, but we will not see the society of 1984. The slogans and

manners of dissident youth around the world are like
a caricature of Summerhill (naturally a caricature because there has not yet been a social change adequate
to domesticate them): participatory democracy, do
your thing, don't trust anybody over thirty, drop out
of the system. Summerhill's affectionate family of autonomous persons is a model for all pads, communes,
and tribes. The sexual freedom exists that Neill
approved but could not legally sanction. Careless dress
has become the common uniform.

Obviously there is something fishy about this beautiful
story, and we cannot let it stand. But first let me answer a
criticism of progressive education that is not justified. It is
said that contemporary progressive education is a gimmick
geared to the middle class—we must remember that Pesta-
lozzi did his work and Montessori her best work with the
outcast. The black community, especially, resents being
used for "experiments." Poor children, it is claimed, need
to learn the conventional ropes so that they can compete for
power in the established system or at least be able to con the
system. Therefore black parents demand "quality education" and expect their children to wear ties.

This criticism is wrongheaded. The scholastic evidence, for instance the *Eight Years Study,* shows that the
more experimental the high school, the more successfully
the graduates compete in conventional colleges when it is
necessary. And so long as black children do not get the same
reward as whites for equal conventional achievement—
though this situation is markedly changing—it is better for
them not to be caught in an unprofitable groove but to have
more emotional freedom, initiative, and flexibility, to be
able to find and make opportunities. More important, I
don't agree with the theory of Head Start, that disadvantaged children need special training for their intellectual
faculties to prepare them for learning. There seems to be
nothing wrong with their intellectual faculties; they have
learned to speak and they can make practical syllogisms very
nicely if they need to and are not thwarted. If black children
do not have the patterns to succeed in school, the plausible

move is to change the school rather than to badger the children; and this has been the program of progressive education. But the trouble might be just the opposite, as Elliott Shapiro has suggested, that these children have been pushed too early to take responsibility for themselves and their little brothers and sisters, and these life problems have been too insoluble to reason about. They can reason but there's no use to it; and they cannot afford to be playful and experimental. It's psychically more economic to be stupid and withdrawn. If so, what the children need is freedom from pressure to perform, and of course better food, more quiet, more privacy, and a less impoverished environment to grow in at their own pace. From this point of view, the schooling should not be more competitive as "quality education," but more like Summerhill.

But what has really been wrong with progressive education is that, in its own terms, its successes have been rather total failures. It has been the harbinger of social change, but the social changes have not paid off as promised or as the visionaries intended. Jacksonian democracy, as described by Tocqueville, was very different from the Old Regime, but it was not the natural nobility of *Émile* or the vision of Jefferson. It lacked especially the good taste, fraternity, and general will that Rousseau hankered after, or the natural aristocracy of Jefferson. Dewey's pragmatic and social-minded conceptions have ended up as the service university, technocracy, labor bureaucracy, suburban togetherness. But Dewey was thinking of workers' management and education for workers' management; and like Frank Lloyd Wright he wanted a functional culture of materials and industrial processes, not glossy Industrial Design and the consumer standard of living.

The likelihood is that A. S. Neill's hope too will be badly realized. It is not hard to envisage a society in the near future in which self-reliant and autonomous people who know nothing will be attendants of a technological apparatus over which they have no control. Indeed, Neill describes with near satisfaction such success stories among his own graduates. Alternately, it is conceivable that an affluent society will accommodate its free-wheeling hippies by supporting them like Indians on a reservation. Their Zen philosophy of *satori* was originally grounded in a violent feudalism, of which it was the spiritual solace, and it could prove so again.

Protecting his free affectionate community, Neill protects it a few years too long, both from the oppressive mechanistic world and from adolescent solitude—it is hard to be alone in Summerhill. And it seems to me there is something inauthentic in Neill's latitudinarian lack of standards, as when he says that Beethoven and rock-and-roll are equivalent, though he prefers Beethoven. Of course, the statement is objectively false, as can be shown by structurally analyzing the music; but besides, he overlooks the historical reality, which I referred to in the preceding chapter—that we are not only free organisms but parts of mankind that has historically made itself with great inspirations and terrible conflicts. We cannot slough off the accumulation of it, however burdensome, without becoming trivial and finally servile. It seems clear by now that the noisy youth subculture is not only not grown-up, which is to the good, but prevents ever being grown-up.

vi

It is arguable that the chief problem in the coming generation will be survival—whether surviving nuclear blasts, genocide, ecological disaster, or mass starvation and endless wars. But if so, this would be the present task of pedagogy. There already exist wilderness schools for self-reliance and it has been proposed that guerrilla warfare be the curriculum in Harlem schools. The delicately interlocking technologies and overgrown cities are indeed terribly vulnerable, and the breakdown could be pretty fatal.

But as I have been saying in this book, I do not believe in this apocalyptic future of the breakdown of civilization. Rather, my own "Reformation" thinking about education is as follows:

(1) Incidental education, taking part in the on-going

activities of society, must again be made the chief means of learning and teaching.

(2) Most high schools should be eliminated, with other kinds of youth communities taking over their sociable functions.

(3) College training should generally follow, rather than precede, entry into the professions.

(4) The chief occupation of educators should be to see to it that the activities of society provide incidental education, rather than exploitation or neglect. If necessary, we must invent new useful activities that offer educational opportunities.

(5) The purpose of elementary pedagogy, through age twelve, should be to delay socialization, to protect children's free growth, since our families and community both pressure them too much and do not attend to them enough. Modern times pollute and waste natural human resources, the growing children, just as they do the land, air, and water. What else could one expect?

Let me review the arguments for this program. We must drastically cut back formal schooling because the present extended tutelage is against nature and arrests growth. The effort to channel the process of growing up according to a preconceived curriculum and method discourages and wastes many of the best human powers to learn and cope. Schooling does not prepare for real performance; it is largely carried on for its own sake. Only a small fraction, the "academically talented"—about 15 percent according to James Conant—thrive in schools without being bored or harmed by them. Schooling isolates the young from the older generation and alienates them.

On the other hand, it makes no sense for many of the brightest and most sensitive young merely to drop out or confront society with hostility. This cannot lead to social reconstruction. The complicated and confusing conditions of modern times need knowledge and fresh thought, and therefore long acquaintance and participation precisely by the young. Young religious enthusiasts imagine that our civilization is about to collapse, so there is no point to acquaintance and participation; but they are in error. Militant radicals seem to think that mere political change will solve the chief problems, or that they will solve themselves after political change, but this also is a delusion. The problems of urbanization, technology, ecology, and world community have not been faced by any political group. The educational systems of other advanced countries are no better than ours, and their young are equally dissenting. Finally, it has been my Aristotelian experience that most people cannot organize their lives without productive activity that is socially approved—though, of course, not necessarily paid activity; and the actual professions, services, industries, arts and sciences are the arena of activity. Doing one's thing and radical politics are careers for very few.

As it is, to be sure, the actual activities of American society either exclude the young, or exploit them, or corrupt them. Here is the task for educators. We must make the rules of licensing and hiring realistic to the actual work and get rid of mandarin requirements. We must design apprenticeships that are not exploitative. Society desperately needs much work that is not now done, both intellectual and manual, in urban renewal, rural reconstruction, ecology, communications, and the arts, and all these could make use of young people. Many activities, like community development and Vocations for Social Change, can be well organized by young people themselves. Little think tanks like the Oceanic Institute at Makapuu Point or the Institute for Policy Studies in Washington, which are not fussy about diplomas, have provided excellent training for the young. There is need for many thousands of centers of design and research, and local newspapers, radio stations, and theaters.

Our aim should be to multiply the paths of growing up, instead of narrowing the one existing school path. There must be opportunity to start again after false starts, to cross over, take a moratorium, travel, work on one's own. To insure freedom of option, so that the young can maintain and express their critical attitude, all adolescents should be guaranteed a living. (The present cost of high school and the first years of college is enough to pay for this.)

Of course, the advantage of making education less academic has occurred to school people too. There are a myriad of programs to open the schools to the world; on the one hand, by importing outside professionals, artists in residence, gurus, mothers, and dropouts as teachers' aides; and on the other hand, by exporting academic credit for work-study, community action, writing novels, service in mental hospitals, junior year abroad, and other kinds of released time. Naturally I am enthusiastic about these developments. I only want the school people to go the small further step of abolishing the present school establishment, instead of using these means to aggrandize it.

There is some talk in the United States (and some actual practice in China and Cuba) about adolescent years being devoted to public service. This is good if the service is not compulsory and regimenting. It is one good option.

It is possible for every education to be tailor-made according to each youth's developing interest and choice. Youthful choices along the way will be very often ill-conceived and wasteful, but they will express desire and immediately meet reality, and therefore they should converge on right vocation more quickly than by any other course. Vocation is what one is good at and can do, what uses a reasonable amount of one's powers, and gives one a useful occupation in a community that is one's own. The right use of the majority of people would make a stable society far more efficient than our own. Some, perhaps many, have peculiar excellences that no social planning can anticipate, but these are more likely to find their own further way if they have had entry into a field where they are competent and are accepted. It was Goethe's wise advice to a young man not to try to do what he wished, which would almost certainly prove to be deceptive, but to get engaged in life by doing something he was competent at and then to seize opportunities that might arise; these would lead to what he more deeply wanted and ought to do.

Those with academic talents can choose academic schools, and such schools are better off unencumbered by the sullen uninterested bodies of the others. But the main use of academic teaching is for those already busy in sciences and professions who need academic courses along the way.

(Cooper Union in New York City used to fulfill this function very well.) And in this context of real motivation, there can finally be the proper use of new pedagogic technology, as a means of learning at one's own time and pace, whereas at present this technology makes the school experience still more rigid and impersonal.

Inevitably, in this set-up, employers would themselves provide ancillary academic training, especially if they had to pay for it anyway, instead of using parents' and taxpayers' money. In my opinion, this ancillary rather than prior schooling would do more than any other single thing to give black, rural, and other "culturally deprived" youth a fairer entry and chance for advancement, since what is to be learned ancillary to the job is objective and functional and does not depend on the abstract school style. On the job, as we have seen, there is no correlation between competence and years of prior schooling.

But with schooling on the job, another problem emerges. Educationally, schooling on the job is usually superior; it has reality and motivation. But the political and moral consequences of such a system are ambiguous. The difficulty is not, as is usually the objection, that such training is narrow, for "comprehensive" schooling does not produce "well-rounded" people either; and if a job does not have humane bearings, perhaps it is not worth doing at all. But on-the-job training does put the young under the control of the employer, whether private, corporate, or state. At present in the United States, a young person is hired on the basis of actual credentials; these have cost him wasted years and they rarely signify any actual skill, but he brings them as his own, he has gotten them elsewhere. This is alienating to him as a person, but it does give him a measure of free-market power, he has something to contract with. If he is to be schooled on the job, however, he must be hired for his promise and attended to as a person. This is less alienating, but it can lead to company paternalism, like Japanese capitalism or like Fidel Castro's Marxist vision of farm- and factory-based schools. On the other hand, if the young have a secure living, have options, and can organize and criticize, on-the-job education is the quickest way to workers' management which, in my opinion, is the only effective industrial democracy.

University education, in the liberal arts and the principles of the professions, is for adults who already know something. Otherwise, as Plato pointed out, it is just verbalizing.

To provide a protective and life-nourishing environment for children up through twelve, Summerhill is an adequate model and can easily be adapted to urban conditions (see Chapter 6), especially if we include houses of refuge for children to resort to, when necessary, to escape parental and neighborhood tyranny or terror. Probably an even better model would be the Athenian pedagogue touring the city with his charges, as I describe in Chapter 10 of *The Empire City;* but for this the streets and working places of the city must be made safer and more available. (The ideal of city planning is for the children to be able to use the city, for no city is governable if it does not grow citizens who feel it is theirs.) The goal of elementary education should be a very modest one: it is for a small child, under his own steam, not on a leash, to be able to poke interestedly into whatever goes on and to be able, by observation, questions, and practical imitation, to get something out of it on his own terms. In our society this happens pretty well at home up to age four, but after that it becomes forbiddingly difficult.

v i i

I have often made this pitch for incidental education, and found no takers. Curiously, I get the most respectful if wistful attention at teachers' colleges, even though what I propose is quite impossible under their auspices. Teachers know how much they are wasting the children's time of life, they are dissatisfied with their own roles, and they understand that my ideas are fairly conservative, whereas our present schooling is a new mushroom.

In general audiences the response is incredulity.

Against all evidence, people are convinced that what we do must make sense or is inevitable. It does not help if I point out that in dollars and cents it might be cheaper, and it would certainly be more productive, in tangible goods and services, to eliminate most schools and, instead, make the community and work more educational. Yet the majority in a general audience are willing to say that they themselves get very little out of their own school years. Occasionally a "reactionary" businessman agrees with me enthusiastically that book-learning isn't worth much; or an old socialist agrees, because he thinks you have to get your books the hard way.

Among radical students I am met with sullen silence. They want Student Power and are unwilling to answer whether they are authentically students at all. That's not where it's at. But in my opinion, instead of Student Power they should be asking for a more open entry into society; they should demand that education money be spent more usefully; they should sit in at the state capitol until licensing is possible without irrelevant diplomas. And of course stop harassment and compulsion. The young do have an authentic demand for young people's power, the right to take part in initiating and deciding the functions of society that concern them, as well as governing their own lives which are nobody else's business. Bear in mind that we are speaking of ages seventeen to twenty-five, when at all other times the young would already have been launched in the world. The young have the right to power because they are numerous and directly affected, and especially because their new point of view is indispensable to coping with changing conditions—they themselves being part of the changing conditions.

Perhaps the chief advantage of incidental education over schooling is that it enables the young to carry on their Movement informed and programmatic, grounded in experience and competence, whereas Student Power, springing from a phony situation, is usually symbolic and often merely spiteful.

Chapter 6

i

A big obstacle to children's learning to read is the school setting in which they have to pick it up. For any learning to be skillful and lasting, it must be or become second-nature, self-motivated; and for this, schooling is too impersonal, standardized, and scheduled. If we tried to teach infants to speak by academic methods in an environment like school, my guess is that many would fail and most would stammer.

The analogy between learning to speak and learning to read is not exact, but it is instructive to pursue it, since, in principle, speaking should be much harder to pick up. As many philosophers have pointed out, learning to speak is a stupendous intellectual achievement, involving the use of signs, acquiring a vocabulary, and mastering an extraordinary kind of algebra, syntax, with almost infinite variables in a large number of sentence forms. Yet almost all succeed equally well, no matter what their class or culture, though they learn a different vocabulary and syntax depending on their class or culture. Every child picks up a dialect, "correct" or "incorrect," adequate to express the thoughts and needs of his milieu.

We do not know, scientifically, how children learn to speak, but we can describe some of the indispensable conditions:

1. The child is constantly exposed to speech related to interesting behavior in which he often shares. ("Now, where's your little coat? We're going to the supermarket. It's cold out today.")
2. The speakers are persons important to the child, and they often single him out to speak to or about him.
3. The child plays with the sounds, tries them out, freely imitates what he hears, approximates it without interference or correction. When he succeeds, he is rewarded by attention and other useful results.
4. Later, the child consolidates by his own will what he has learned. He promotes himself or graduates, so to speak, as an accomplished speaker, by leaving his grown-up first teachers. From age three to five he acquires style, accent, and fluency by speaking with his peers, adopting their uniform but also asserting his own tone. He speaks peer speech more than parent speech, but he is uniquely recognizable as speaking in his own voice and way.

We can infer the "naturalness" or normalcy of this process from the derangements that occur when conditions are amiss. If the parents are mute, the infant does not learn to speak. If there is demand and expectation, a common result is stuttering. If there is emotional disturbance in other functions of growing up, like being weaned, there may be certain speech defects, like lisping. If the parents instill a middle-class self-consciousness (guiltiness), the syntax abounds in the use of "I" and indirect discourse. In a "culture of poverty," there are few complex sentences, and physical nudging and hitting occur instead of growth of vocabulary. (Wordsworth observed the cultural conditions of good and bad speech perhaps better than anybody else.

Now suppose, by contrast, that we tried to teach speaking by academic methods in a school setting:

1. Speaking would be a curricular subject abstracted from the web of activity and reserved for special hours punctuated by bells. It might even be forbidden for nonprofessionals to talk to the infants,

since this would interfere with the proper method.

2. Speaking would be a tool subject rather than a way of being in the world.

3. It would not spring from the child's needs in immediate situations but would be taught according to the teacher's idea of his future advantage, perhaps aiming at his getting a job sixteen years later, or being admitted to an elite college.

4. Along the way, therefore, the child would have to be "motivated," the exercises would have to be "fun." In order to make up for the skimpiness of experience in the classroom, it might be wise to provide audio-visual aids.

5. The lessons would be arranged in a graded series from simple to complex. It would be generally held that learning monosyllables precedes polysyllables. Some would hold that words precede sentences and must be mastered first; others would hold that sentences precede words. Perhaps the Head Start curriculum would be devoted to the phonemes, in order to assure later articulateness or the first hour should specialize in nouns, the second in verbs. The second semester could put these together.

6. The teacher's relation to the infant would be further depersonalized by the need to speak or listen to only what suits two dozen other children as well.

7. Being continually called on, corrected, tested, and evaluated to meet a standard in a group, some children would become stutterers. Others would devise a phony system of apparently speaking in order to get by; the speech would mean nothing. Others would balk at being processed and would purposely become stupid. Some of these would get remedial courses. Others would play hooky and go to special infant jails.

8. Since there is a predetermined range of what can be spoken and how it must be spoken—decided ultimately in the state capital or according to the guidelines of the National Science Foundation—

everybody's speech would be standard and unlike any native dialect. (You can hear this exotic product among principals in the New York City school system.) Expression of the child's own experience or feeling would be discouraged by various kinds of negative conditioning.

These eight disastrous conceptions are not an unfair caricature of how we teach reading. Reading is treated as abstract, instrumental, irrelevant to actual needs, extrinsically motivated, impersonal, standardized, not expressive of truth or art. The teaching often produces awkwardness, faking, and balking. Let me also make a few further points, specific to reading.

1. Omitting their prima facie functions as reminders, signs, communication with absent persons, self-expression, and studied formulation, writing and reading are astoundingly divorced from the speaking which is their matrix. Teachers of freshman English in colleges discover that, for the majority of the students, writing and reading have no intrinsic relation to saying and hearing; especially writing —"compositions"—is a tortured song and dance that has no connection with saying something or having something to say. Speech too has been ossified. It is really necessary to unteach everything and go back to psychosomatic exercises in babbling, free association, and saying and writing dirty words. And young people consider it quite plausible when McLuhan and others say that writing and reading will pass away, as if mankind were going to give up talking as the primary way of communicating, expressing themselves, and being in the world. But people are going to go on talking and, hopefully, writers will continue to renew speech.

2. Most people who have learned to read and write fluently have done so on their own, with their own material, whether library books, newspapers, comic books, or street signs. They may, or may not, have picked up the ABC's in school, but they acquired skill, and preserved what they had learned, on their own. This self-learning is important, for it is not at the mechanical level of ABC's that reading retardation drastically occurs, but in the subsequent years

when the good readers are going it alone, and the others are either signing off and forgetting, or settling for a vestigial skill that makes it impossible for them ever to read an authentic book.

3. According to some neurophysiologists, given the exposure to written code in modern urban and suburban conditions, any emotionally normal child in middle-class surroundings will spontaneously learn to read by age nine, just as he learned to speak by age three. It is impossible for him not to pick up the code unless he is systematically interrupted and discouraged, for instance by trying to teach him in school.

Of course, children of the culture of poverty do not have the ordinary middle-class need for literacy and the premium put on it, and they are less exposed to it among their parents and peers. Thus for these children there is a use for the right kind of schooling.

4. Against my argument here, it seems that in all modern countries school methods, lessons, copying, and textbooks, have been used successfully to teach children to read. But this evidence is deceptive. High competence was expected of very few—e.g., in 1900 in the United States only 6 percent graduated from high school. Little effort was made with children of the working class, and none at all with those from the culture of poverty. It is inherently unlikely that the same procedures could work with the present change of scale and population. Where a dramatic effort has been made to teach adults to read, en masse, as in Cuba, the method has been informal, "each one teach one."

5. Also, the experience of freshman English shows that achieving a test score adequate for college entrance does not prove much. John Holt has described, in a good middle-class high school, the subtle devices that are learned to get by; for this is the real life problem, not reading and writing. The case is analogous to the large group among Puerto Rican children in New York who apparently speak English well but who in fact cannot say anything that they need or mean, such as "Pass the salt" or "My friend is in jail." They are just putting on a performance. But unless reading serves for truth and art, why bother? We have seen that it's not

much use on most jobs, except for getting hired. Radio, television, and movies give other satisfactions more easily.

i i

Is it possible and feasible to teach reading somewhat in the way children learn to speak, by intrinsic interest, with personal attention, and in an environment less isolated from life than our schools? Pedagogically and economically it is possible. The following was roughly the model for the First Street School on the Lower East Side in New York City; and the cost there was approximate to that in the New York public schools, $900 per child at that time. Politically, however, such a solution is unlikely, since it threatens both vested interests and popular prejudices.

For ages six to eleven, I propose a system of tiny schools, radically decentralized. By decentralization I here do not mean "community control"—which is a political good that I have been urging for twenty years—but decentralization to the level of actual operation: a mini-school would have about twenty-eight children and four teachers, and each tiny school would be largely administered by its own staff and parents, with considerable say also by the children, as in Summerhill.

The four teachers are:

1. A teacher licensed and salaried as in the present system. Since the present average class size is twenty-eight, these are available.
2. A graduating college senior from one of the local colleges, perhaps embarking on graduate study. Salary $2000. There is no lack of candidates, young people who want to do something useful and interesting in a free setting.
3. A literate housewife and mother, who can also prepare lunch. Salary $4000. Again there is no lack of candidates.
4. A literate, willing, and intelligent high school grad-

uate or dropout. Salary $2000. No lack of candi-
dates.

The staff, in New York City, should be black, white,
and Puerto Rican. And it is the case, demonstrated by the
First Street School, that in a small set-up, with children
getting individual attention, it is easy to have mixed classes.
Middle-class parents, at least in New York, do not withdraw
when they do not fear that their children will be swamped
and retarded. Black parents can be persuaded that the set-up
is useful for the children. Spanish-speaking children will
come if their friends come.

For its setting, the mini-school would occupy two,
three, or four rooms in existing school buildings or church
basements and settlement houses otherwise empty during
school hours, rooms set aside in housing built by public
funds, and rented storefronts. The layout is fairly indifferent, since a major part of activity would occur outside
the place. The place should be able to be transformed into
a clubhouse, decorated and equipped according to the
group's own decision. It is good to be on the street where
the children live so that they can come and go at will; but
there is also an advantage in locating in racial and ethnic
border areas, to increase the chance of intermixture. For
purposes of assembly, health services, and some games, ten
tiny schools can unite and use present public school facilities.

The cost saving would be the almost total elimination
of top-down administration and the kind of special services
that are required because of size and rigidity. The chief uses
of central administration would be funding, licensing, finding sites, and some inspection. There would be no principals
and assistants, secretaries and assistants. Curriculum, texts,
equipment are to be decided as needed—and despite the
present putative economies of scale, they would be cheaper,
since less is pointless or wasted; and the second-hand and
hand-me-down is quite adequate. Record keeping would be
at a minimum. There is no need for truant officers when a
teacher-and-six call at the absentee's home and inquire.
There is little need for remedial personnel, since the staff

and parents are always in contact and the whole enterprise can be regarded as remedial. Studies of large top-down directed enterprises, in which persons are the main cost, show that the total cost is invariably at least 300 percent above the cost of the function, in this case the interaction of teachers, children, and parents. We here would put this 300 percent saving into increasing the number of grownups and diversifying the possibilities of experience. Finally in the conditions of big city real estate, there is great advantage in fitting schools into available niches rather than building $4 million school buildings.

This model permits natural learning of reading. There can be exposure to activities of the city. A teacher-and-seven can spend most of the time on the streets, in a playground, visiting business offices, watching television, at a museum, chatting with the corner druggist, riding the buses and subways, visiting rich and poor homes. Such experiences are saturated with speaking, reading and writing. For instance, a group might choose to spend several weeks at the Museum of Natural History, re-labeling the exhibits for their own level of comprehension; and the curator would be well advised to allot them a couple of hundred dollars to do it.

Each child can be addressed according to his own style and interests in choice of reading matter. Given so many contexts, a teacher can easily strike when the iron is hot, whether reading the destination of a bus or the label on a can of soup. If some children catch on quickly and forge ahead on their own, the teacher need not waste their time and can concentrate on the others. The setting does not prejudge as to formal or informal techniques, phonics, Montessori, rote drill, Moore's typewriter, labeling the furniture, or any other method.

As a writer, I like Sylvia Ashton-Warner's method of teaching little Maoris to read. Each day she tried to catch the most passionate concern of each child as he came in, and to give him a card with that key word—usually the words were those of fear, anger, hunger, loneliness, sexual desire. Soon each child had a large, ineradicable, and very peculiar reading list, not at all like *Dick and Jane*. He would then easily progress to reading and writing anything.

From the beginning, in this method, reading and writing are gut-meaningful; they express truth and feeling.

The ragged administration by children, staff, and parents is pedagogically a virtue, since this too is real and can be saturated with reading and writing, writing down the arguments, the rules, the penalties. It gives a chance for some objective communication between parent and child.

For the first five school years there is no merit in the standard curriculum. To repeat Dewey's maxim, for a small child everything in the environment is educative if he attends to it with guidance. In any case, normal children can learn the standard eight years' curriculum in about four months, at age twelve.

And there is little merit, for this age, in the usual teacher-training. Any literate and well-intentioned grown-up or late teen-ager knows enough to teach a small child many things. Teaching small children is a difficult art; we do not know how to train the improvisational genius it requires, and the untrained may or may not have it: compare one mother with another, or one big sister or brother with another. Since at this age one teaches the child, not the subject, the relevant art is psychotherapy, and the most useful course for a teacher's college is probably a group therapy in order that the aspirant teachers become aware of themselves. It is also useful to have a course in the economics and politics of the school establishment. And the history and philosophy of education is a beautiful subject.

The chief criterion for selecting a staff is the one I have mentioned: liking children and being willing to be attentive to them. But given this setting, which they can more or less run as they will, many young people would go into teaching and continue, whereas in the New York system the annual turnover approaches 20 percent after years of wasted training and an elaborate routine of testing and hiring.

iii

In my opinion, there is too much fuss about primary education altogether, and of course that is part of its difficulty. On classroom visits as a member of a school board, I was continually puzzled as to why they were doing what they were doing, making themselves so much trouble; and there was so much needless constraint and suffering. Yet the teachers were failing to give the attention and common courtesy that they would spontaneously have given the same children outside of that school building. Really, all that is necessary—but it *is* necessary—is pleasant baby-sitting and attention by the community of grown-ups but this is what our society so notoriously fails to provide. I am sure that the above proposal, which I prepared for hearings on reading before the borough president of Manhattan, is itself too complicated. Many groups of parents could make still simpler arrangements to suit their needs.

Yet the political obstacles to these ideas seem to be in-superable. First, the school administration, with its builders and suppliers, does not intend to go largely out of business. And it must see any radical decentralization as impossible to administer and dangerous, for everything cannot then be controlled. Some child is bound to break a leg and the in-surance companies will not cover. Some teen-ager is bound to be indiscreet and the *Daily News* will explode in head-lines.

The teachers' union does not like to devalue pro-fessional perquisites and to see the schools flooded with the unlicensed, even though, as I have been careful to provide, no teacher would lose a job. And broken to the public school harness, experienced teachers consider free and in-ventive teaching to be impossible and unprofessional.

But most fatally, poor parents—who are the most ag-grieved by the present schools and are politically on the rampage—tend to regard unrigidly structured education as downgrading, as not taking the children seriously, using them for experiments, and also as vaguely immoral. Mili-tant Black Power people object to the racial mixture. (But children, Kant said, must be educated for the future better society, which, in my Enlightenment bias, cannot be sep-aratist.)

However, the dissatisfaction with the schools is so serious that there are bound to be extraordinary changes.

Perhaps some governments will try giving the school money directly to the parents, as Milton Friedman recommends. Or they might pay for schools set up by small groups of parents, as is an option in Denmark. In such cases, the First Street School is a good urban model.

Chapter 7

i

Nevertheless, there is something deeply unsatisfying in the educational program I have just outlined. I think I have plausibly shown how we can stop trying to process the young according to our preconceptions and yet open our world for them. (Whether we do or not is a political matter —and we had better.) But if we consider how alienated they are, as I have also tried to show, it seems unlikely that they will *move* into that world, even though on their own terms, even though it is advantageous, and even though it is by and large the only world there is. Why should they be rational?

Making an educational proposal is like designing an intentional community. One provides for the physical, economic, social, and psychological needs of the members hopefully better than in ordinary society. Yet the overwhelming evidence of all such places is that they do not survive unless there is some nonrational motive, religious or nationalist or pacifist, that makes them have to survive. A community finally has to have its own poetry. Now, the alienated young at present do have their own poetry—it is occasionally pretty good but small, it is usually poor—but they certainly don't have our poetry, and in fact very few of them can read English.

So I must go back to a very old-fashioned topic of educational theory, how to transmit Culture with a big C, the greatness of Man, for unless they want to continue our history, there is no point in their assuming our world. This topic is no longer discussed by conventional educators and it was never much discussed by progressive educators, though Dewey took it increasingly seriously in his later years. In our generation, however, it is a critical problem, and I cannot think of a way to solve it. But it is useful to try to define it.

To carry on a going society, I have been arguing, most transmission can be accomplished by incidental education. The physical environment and social culture force themselves on us, and the young are bound to grow up to them well or badly. Whatever is going on always fundamentally determines the curriculum in formal schooling; and if there is no schooling at all, it is the focus of children's attention and interest anyway, it is what is there. Dewey's maxim is a good one: there is no need to bother about curriculum, for whatever a child turns to is potentially educative and, with good management, one thing leads to another. Even skills that are considered essential prerequisites, like reading, will be learned spontaneously in normal urban and suburban conditions.

But humane culture is not what is obviously there for a child, and in our times it is unusually lacking. Decently confused, parents go easy on moral instruction. In the environment there is little spirit of a proud tradition, with heroes and martyrs. There is a plethora of concerts and records, art museums and planetariums, children's encyclopedias, and academic courses in art appreciation and general science, but the disinterested ideals of science and art are hardly mentioned, and do not seem to operate publicly. The sacredness of those ideals no longer exists even on college campuses. As we have seen, almost no young person of college age believes there are autonomous professionals or has heard of such a thing. Great souls of the past do not speak to a young person as persons like himself once he learns their language, nor does he bother to learn their language. The old conflicts of history do not seem to him to have been human conflicts, so they too are of no interest.

It is said that, except for school courses, intellectual young people read astoundingly few books, and they themselves attribute their lack of interest to the more immediate appeal of movies, radio, and television, and the quick news in periodicals.* But my guess is that the causation is the other way. Memory is the mother of the Muses. The literary process—and it is the same with the other fine arts—is a blend of tradition and immediate excitement, syllogism and observation, learning and metaphor. When there is no sense of history, the nuances and complexities of literature seem to have no content; they are irrelevant and boring. The young, finally, simply cannot follow a history-rich and organic motion of thought, a book, and they take it to be a mechanical train of sentences. They are sensitive enough to the nuances in a movie or the particularities of the ludicrous in a TV commercial, but these depend on experiences that they and their friends have had in their own lifetimes.

Since the mass pitch of TV, records, and movies cuts down the possibility of using unexpected sentences even more, finally the only way to communicate anything particular is to rely on the various inflections of grunts and exclamations, like a dozen levels of saying "Wow," or on nonverbal means altogether. So Marshall McLuhan's prediction of the end of literature comes true, though not for the reason he imagines. Like McLuhan, the young do not understand that writing is better speech, not stupider speech. Going to college doesn't seem to help this. Mass higher education certainly makes it worse.

The young have strong feelings for frankness, loyalty, fairness, affection, freedom, and other virtues of generous natures. They quickly resent the hypocrisy of politicians, administrators, and parents who mouth big abstractions and act badly or pettily. But in fact, they themselves—like most politicians and administrators and many parents—

---

* I have read statistics to this effect in the *New York Times* in interviews with intellectual leaders of the hippies. Against them, my publisher mentions the large number of books sold, including mine. My experience, however, has been that the larger the (paperback) collection in a pad, the more virgin are the books. To buy the books is part of making the scene.

seem to have forgotten the concrete reality of ideals like magnanimity, compassion, honor, consistency, civil liberty, integrity, justice though the heavens fall, and unpalatable truth, all of which are not gut feelings and are often not even pragmatic but are maintained to create and re-create Mankind and the possibility of the Second Coming. Naturally, without these ideals and their always possible and often actual conflict, there is no tragedy. Most young persons I have met seem to disbelieve that tragedy exists; they interpret impasse as timidity and casuistry as finking out. And they are quite ready to call something bullshit just because they don't dig it (I think they learned this in sensitivity workshops).

Their ignorance has advantages. The bother with transmitting humane culture is that it must be re-created in spirit or it is a dead weight upon present spirit, and then it does produce timidity, pedantry, and hypocrisy. And then it is better forgotten. Certainly the attempt to teach it by courses in school, or by sermons like this, is a disaster. Presumably it was kept going by the living example of a large number of people who took it seriously and leavened society; but the Western tradition has not recommended itself in my or my parents' generations.

The logical way to teach the humanities would be for some of us to picket the TV studios in despair to bear witness to our cause. But we are tired. And anyway, when we have done similar things, students have put their own rather different interpretation on our action. For instance, when we try to purge the university of military projects, students attack scientific research itself because that could be abused —and is even bound to be abused—as if science were not necessarily a risky adventure. They don't see that this is a tragic dilemma. They seem quite willing—though battening on it in the United States—to write off Western civil law.

Yet, apart from the spirit congealed in them, we do not really have our sciences and arts, professions and civic institutions. It is inauthentic merely to use the products and survivals, and I don't think we can in fact work Western civilization without its vivifying tradition. Later in this book I will return to the thought that the simplest reason the cities are ungovernable is that there aren't enough citizens; this happened during the Roman Empire too.

It is conceivable that the so-called Third World can adapt our technology and reinterpret it according to other ideals. So some of the militant students say, and this was supposed to be the theme of the conference in Havana against Cultural Imperialism. But I read dozens of the papers delivered there, and I did not find a single new proposition. Anyway, this does nothing for us. Here at home it is poignant what marvels some people expect from the revival of African masks.

I have previously mentioned a young hippie—it was at Esalen—singing a song attacking the technological way of life, but he was on lysergic acid and strumming an electric guitar plugged into the infrastructure of California. The poem was a pastiche of surrealism and E. E. Cummings, but the rhythm and harmony came right out of the Smoky Mountains. I couldn't make anybody see why this wouldn't do.

I tried to make clear to a young lady at the Antioch-Putney School of Education that a child has a historical right to know that there is a tie between Venus and the sun—I showed it to her—and thanks to Isaac Newton we know its equation, which is even more beautiful than the Evening Star itself. It is not a matter of choice whether he ought to know this or not. Yet she was right, for if it's not his thing, it's pointless to show it to him, as it was to her.

Another time Stokely Carmichael was sounding off (into a microphone) about the whites—this was at the Dialectics of Liberation in London—and I asked him if Galileo was white, if that was a plausible thing to say about Galileo. For some reason that defeats me, this question made him angry.

But it won't do. It won't do. Willfully ignorant of the inspiration and grandeur of our civilization, though somewhat aware of its brutality and terror, the young are patsies for the "inevitabilities" of modern times. They no longer know what to claim as their own and what to attack as the enemy. Omitting Prometheus, Faraday, Edison, the longing of mankind for light and energy, they are left with Consolidated Edison owning the field, and themselves saying, "Shut it down." If they cannot take on our only world appreciatively and very critically, they can only confront her or be servile to her, and then she is too powerful for any of us.

Margaret Mead says, truly, that young people in modern times are like native sons, whereas we others use the technology gingerly and talk like the foreign-born. I am often pleased at how competent my young friend proves to be; my apprehension for him is usually groundless. But he is swamped by presentness. Since there is no background or structure, everything is equivalent and superficial. He can repair the TV but he thinks the picture is real (Marshall McLuhan doesn't help). He says my lecture blew his mind and I am flattered till he tells me that L. Ron Hubbard's metempsychosis in Hellenistic Sardinia blew his mind. I wonder if he has any mind to blow.

I sometimes have an eerie feeling that there are, around the world, a few dozen of Plato's guardians, ecologists, and psychosomatic physicians, who with worried brows are trying to save mankind from destroying itself. This is a sorry situation for Jeffersonian anarchists like myself who think we ought to fend for ourselves and are competent to do so. The young are quick to point out the mess we have made, but I don't see that they really care about that, as if it were not their mankind also. Rather, I see them with the Christmas astronauts, flying toward the Moon and looking back at the earth shining below: it is as if they are about to abandon an old house and therefore it makes no difference if they litter it with beer cans. These are bad thoughts.

i i

Having said thus much about the vandals, however, let me speak of a contrasting experience of education that I have occasionally had in the draft-resistance movement.

The resisters are exceptionally virtuous young men and they are understandably earnest about the fix they are in, which makes them liable to two to five years in jail. Then, in conversation with them, if they are guided by a few Socratic questions, they come to remember the ideas of Allegiance, Sovereignty, Legitimacy, Exile, and bitter Patriotism, all of which cannot be conveyed in college courses in political science. It is a model of incidental learning of the humanities. I am uneasy to generalize from it—must the alienated enter extreme situations in order to revive the sane and classical?

Maybe so. If the humanities—the achievement of value by the occurrence of spirit in communities and individuals through the long centuries—if they are indeed how man has appointed himself and has become, then they will surely emerge and operate in extreme situations. What is necessary is to be for real in one's present plight, which is bound to be historical, willy-nilly, and the ancient humanities will come to the rescue to make sense of it. No doubt this is solid comfort; but it is a hectic kind of schooling that I would not urge on anybody.

This may be the simplest explanation of the revival of old images in historical crises, Brutus during the French Revolution, Hebrew patriarchs during the Reformation, the Reformers themselves, whom I now keep alluding to. An old tradition serves as a second line of defense to which alienated people can repair; and it is there to repair to; just as in psychotherapy, when a patient lets go of a neurotic present adjustment he remembers or acts out archaic behavior from the last time he made sense. It is his integrity. And great poets, who are always somewhat alien in the world that does not make enough sense—Homer, Shakespeare, the poets of Roland and the Cid—celebrate virtues outdated in their times.

But the most hopeful way of looking at the problem, how to transmit humane culture, is as follows. If the institutions of society are made vital and functional and the young can take on those institutions as their own, identify with them, be free in them, participate in their manage-

ment rather than as hired hands, then they will have
learned the humane culture. For, as I put it on the last
page of *The Community of Scholars,*

> Civilization has been a continual gift of the Creator
> Spirit; it consists of inventions, discoveries, insights,
> art works, highly theorized methods of workmanship.
> All of this has vastly accumulated over the ages and
> become very unwieldy, yet, in the spirit, it is always
> appropriable. As Socrates would have said, its mean-
> ing can be recalled. The advantage of recalling it is
> that we are then not enslaved to it, we are citizens.

And the converse must be true. If the institutions are such
that there is entry into them and freedom is possible in
them, the young will pick up their principles. The humanities are not obvious in the environment, but they are the
causes that make it a good environment. It is not that good
institutions make possible a good educational system; they
are the good educational system.

Chapter 8

During the past twenty years, there have been a couple of hundred works of "social criticism" of American ways. One is reminded of the *cahiers* to the States General before the French Revolution, which showed, according to Tocqueville, that not a single activity of French society was viable. A score of our *cahiers* have been pretty good books. In my opinion, the writers may fairly be compared to the *philosophes* of the eighteenth century, or to the humanists of the fifteenth and sixteenth centuries. They are men of letters, using the peculiar method of literature in times of political and religious crisis.

No doubt the older worthies had their own frustrations. At present, the plight of a man of letters is made hard by the following state of affairs: Those in power "co-opt" the critics, manage them so they are rendered ineffectual. (There is little direct censorship.) We are invited to be on panels or even task forces, to represent our way-out views so the proceedings are well rounded; but, speaking for myself, I do not find that my critical insights are taken into account in any actions that ensue. The numerous and dynamic young do take the social critics seriously; indeed, the bulk of their libraries and many of their slogans come from them, and they are eager to act out what they have read. But they cannot read very well; they have been so alienated from history, the professions, and even the nature of things that they do not understand what a humanist is saying. And there is a prevailing sentiment that literature itself is unimportant. It is mere entertainment, or confused sociology or psychiatry, or the posture of a now shabby gentility. New media have made letters moribund and they will pass away. What is useful in them is only a noisy code that must be refined, by other than writers, for purposes of science, technology, and social engineering.

Nevertheless, literature is humanly important. It is odd to have to say this—I first made these remarks at a meeting of the Modern Language Association!—but evidently each era must write its own Defense of Poesy. Literature is not a "linear" unrolling of printed sentences and it is not a crude code; it is artful speech. And speech is not merely a means of communication and expression, as the anthropologists say, but is a chief action in our human way of being in the world. And *pace* Marshall McLuhan, people will continue to speak for the indefinite future, as a chief way of being in the world. (The only alternative hypothesis is that technologists wire their brains; but at this point we would cease to classify them as human beings.)

Psychiatrists of aphasia, from Hughlings Jackson and Head to Kurt Goldstein, have shown that speech is a way of coping with the stream of experience and saves us from the catastrophic all-or-nothing reactions of aphasics. Speech is a peculiar use of symbols that both tell experience and are a substitute for experience, and the manner of speaking is how one is having his experience. To speak to someone not only communicates but creates community; for example, one can signal "Come" by snapping his fingers, but if he says it in words he makes the other into a person. To speak, as Buber and Kafka have said, is in itself a primordial prayer to God and man. Passing from infancy actualizes and defines the self of a growing child; learning to speak is coincidental with, maybe the same as, the formation of the ego. And from Aristotle to Benjamin Whorf and the linguistic analysts, philosophers have repeatedly interpreted vocabulary and grammar as basic hypotheses and world-views of reality.

All this is heightened by literature, oral and written.

The habits, genres, and tropes that have been developed in the long worldwide literary tradition constitute a method of coping with reality different from science, religion, political power, or common sense, but involved with them all. (In my opinion, literature, although it is a method *sui generis,* is not a specialized department of learning but a good way of being in any department. It is a part of philosophy, which as a whole has no department.)

Literature brings to conscious awareness the folk wisdom that exists in vocabulary and grammar. It combines the subjectivity of personal experience and the objectivity of shared experience. Syntax—tenses, voices, moods, direct and indirect discourse, simple and complex sentences—is character, the pattern of one's involvement in experience and with the others; it is a better diagnostic than Rorschach cards. Points of view, what the ancients called "manner," are experiments in phenomenology. Rhythm—regular meter and the rhythm that modifies meter—is feeling; it is one's way of breathing, and being calm, forceful, or languid. Plot structures and chains of syllogism extend our attention span and domesticate experience by reconstructing it with a philosophical beginning, middle, and end. Metaphor is surprise.

The ability of literature to combine memory and learning with present observation and spontaneous impulse remarkably serves the nature of man as the animal who makes himself; for it revives the spirit of past makings, so they are not a dead weight, and yet is a making that is occurring now. Put psychotherapeutically, this process alleviates "inner conflict" and helps heal past trauma by bringing it into the public world of sharable speech.

The materials of literature are cheap and common. This is so with all the fine arts; they are made of mud, rock, gestures, tinkling, and babbling. Those who hanker after multimedia and overwhelming environmental effects should consider what is lost by using an expensive technology. Maybe only a simple and poor medium is flexible and subtle enough to lure the inward outward.

Yet, despite its open access, literature is not democratic but aristocratic. Like any method, it lives by its own tradition as well as social causes or individual ability. But compared with other elites, the Republic of Letters has been a career open to talents, and often classless. I venture to say that a disproportionate number of its stars have been persons socially despised—outcasts, convicts. There is truth in what Wordsworth said, that the speech of the poor and unschooled, if they have been brought up among beautiful scenes and simple affections—or if, I would add, they have been daring and passionate—*is* more literary than the speech of courts and capitalists. Recently Basil Bernstein made some interesting studies of the differences in vocabulary, syntax, and attitude between lower-class and middle-class speech; and Wordsworth's model, as I judge, has the good points of each and avoids the defects of each; it is simply better human speech than that of either Bernstein's cockneys or bourgeois.

The sentences and stances of poets and men of letters have always seemed to provide an independent source or validation in ethics. Moral philosophers have cited them as evidence. In the Book of Job, for instance, the arguments of Whirlwind are logically no more cogent than the other arguments, but their poetry compels assent. (I interpret the beginning of the story to mean that Job is an obsessional neurotic, who can be cured only by being emotionally swept off his feet.) The Italians of the Renaissance used to say that only Eloquence, noble rhetoric, yields the "real" truth, just as only the real truth makes a man eloquent. The aim of literature is "to move and instruct;" in the later formulations of Dryden, this means that literature instructs *by* moving, by disturbing rigid or stereotyped responses. In our own time, Genet says it best when he confesses that his style soars only when he is describing his delinquents, so he knows they are good people; for he is a writer, and writing is his existential act and source of valuation.

So much for the praise of letters, the warrant by which a man of letters can be a social critic. Let me return to his present difficulties.

It is increasingly hard to fulfill one of the elementary functions of writers, to renew the speech of the tribe as it inevitably degenerates. (Confucius said that speech reform was the first step of social change; these days I would sooner get rid of the atom bombs and the pollution, but maybe it's all the same.) The trouble is that the rate of revolutionary change in important aspects of our culture, e.g. urbanization, travel, schooling, communications, militarization, space exploration, is so rapid that it is impossible for any renewal of speech to mature and be assimilated. Good tendencies appear, but they are swamped by the flood of publications. The overall public style is wildly eclectic.

In principle, the omnipresent and seductive TV could have a good or bad influence—as the Canadian Broadcasting Corporation has, for better or worse, standardized the French of young Canadians. But the mode of operation of American TV and other mass media makes them almost necessarily corrupting. Since they aim for big audiences that have few serious interests in common, the subjects treated are trivial or trivialized; communication is quick and superficial; feeling is sensational or bland—or somehow both. Brought up on this fare, young people become adept at judging the nuances and absurdities of TV commercials, but are quite unable to grasp other style or content. They, and most other Americans, cannot hear a line of reasoning if the premises are at all unexpected. Instead of assuming that the writer is saying something different, and trying to figure it out, they decide that he is a bad writer. If the conclusion is not either of the two sides that an issue is supposed to have, they take the argument to be fuzzy. An editor of *Esquire* objected to a line of argument in an article of mine because "the reader would have to think about that"—too much to expect of anybody.

The surface of writing becomes swift and flashy, "cinematic"—the arresting lead, the startling statistic, the apt illustration; but the motion of intellect becomes excruciatingly slow; there must not be more than one poor thought to a page, for the readers cannot follow. An editor of *Harper's Magazine* objected to a piece of mine because it had three ideas; "An article in *Harper's*," he said, "cannot have more than two ideas."

Partisan feelings make it hard to read a sentence. In

editing this book, my editor at Random House, who can usually read English, angrily objected that I was grossly unfair to the young and I called their music worthless. But my intention was to say that the youth subculture, including the music, was a mixed bag. Our quarrel came down to the sentence: "Although the ubiquitous guitars and mountain harmony are phony—in fact, they were invented by the Stalinists in the thirties as a ploy of the Popular Front—electrifying the guitars and playing on the microphones are indigenous." "Oh," the editor said suddenly, "you mean to say '*even* though,' not 'although.'" The circumstances were that he was about to go to Chicago to report the ghastly trial of the eight "conspirators."

For sufficient reasons, it seems to me, the young do not believe in or understand the Western tradition; but then the memory that is alive in humane letters is lost on them, either its allusions or its continuing dialogue millennia old. When I speak at a college, I pepper the discussion with references to Spinoza, Beethoven, and Milton, hoping that the students will learn that former great men were real human beings, but the poignant effect is that they regard me wistfully because I seem to have a past, and they are more forlorn than ever. If I try to analyze a text in its own terms, to find a human spirit coping with its particulars and *therefore* relevant to us, it is taken as an irrelevant exercise in order to avoid present gut issues. Naturally, inability to read a book is cumulative. Since there is no belief in the tradition nor habituation in its ways, it becomes a chore just to read the sentences, and why bother?

Ironically, the stepped-up schooling is literarily disastrous. Librarians have complained to me that children no longer have the time to browse and choose what interests them; I venture to say that very few who can read and write ever learned it by assigned lessons. Literature is both too complicated and too freewheeling to be followed without spontaneous attention springing from desire.

Without doubt, writers and readers can be encumbered by too much traditional baggage, as I myself am. This can prevent primary literature, coping with the existential plight of the person and his community. In my own case

(I guess) I am too lonely to be real—I often remind
of Hawthorne. Yet, starting from scratch, without
tradition altogether, writing and reading are imbe
trivial; ancient errors are tiresomely repeated; p
are taken for ideas; hard-won distinctions are lost
genres have to be reinvented, like reinventing shoe
to boil water. This is boring. When, unencumbere
tory, the young are discussing their immediate re
lems, e.g. the draft, their rapping is fresh, direct, acc
and inventive, excellently literary. When they are discu
politics, institutions, or professions, they become abst
and brassy. When the task is critical judgment or poe
affirmation of their own experience, they are embarrassed
and inarticulate, or they say nothing but clichés.

Needless to say, the lapse of a common background is
grueling for a writer. He has to explain too much, beginning with academic synopses of first principles that he
ought to be able to take for granted. This present essay is
an example: speaking to professors of modern languages, I
start off with a lecture to prove that speech and writing are
good for something. It is like treatises of the fifth century
that commence with Adam and Eve and ultimately get to
the point—I *hope* that this analogy is not accurate.

Most painful is the need to repeat myself. I have written ten books of social theory and social criticism, trying to
explore different relations of man and environment. But
since there is no continuing community of readers and I do
not know what I can take for granted, in each book I have
to establish my point of view and say things I have said before. Impatiently, to get it over with as quickly as possible,
I have written some really hideous paragraphs of sociological and psychological jargon, as a kind of shorthand.

I have found that being misread can have boring
consequences. For instance, in *The Community of Scholars*
I criticized present university administration and pointed
out that a school of ten professionals and a hundred and
fifty students—the equivalent of most medieval schools—
could provide professional education better and more
cheaply than what we now have. So I suggested that some
professors secede and try it. Somehow this made me the

father, or Dutch uncle, of the Free Universities, and since I am sympathetic to the Movement in general, I have had to take part also in the Free Universities. Their curriculum is the psychedelic experience, sensitivity training, the liberation of women, and Castro's Cuba, which are fine subjects but not the law, medicine, and engineering I had in mind.

More serious in life-consequences for writers is the bland hypocrisy of those in power. When we are treated as court jesters or, worse, when our sentences are cadged for purposes that are the opposite of what we intend, then just to maintain our integrity we have to follow up with acts that go beyond our skill or desire: picketing, civil disobedience, raising bail. I have written more leaflets and sat at more press conferences than I like to remember. In order to say my say to the National Security Industries and be paid attention to, I had to summon students to picket the auditorium of the State Department. Writers and scholars spend long hours plotting with their fellows about ways to make trouble, like Hallowe'en goblins.

At any time, also, the contempt for ideas can turn into direct censorship or the chilling climate of blacklisting. Consider the recent disclosure of blacklisting by the Department of Health, Education, and Welfare of scholars who actively opposed the Vietnam war. I can conceive of people honorably indecisive and silent about the policy of the Vietnam war, but it is hard to conceive of anybody talented in community medicine or the education of children or the welfare of the poor who would not be vehemently opposed to that policy. Thus, the effect of the blacklist was to doom the department to mediocrity.

As a poet, I do not have these problems (though plenty of others). On the advice of Longinus, I "write it for Homer, for Demosthenes," and other pleasant company who somehow are more alive to me than most of my contemporaries, though unfortunately not available for comment. Anyway, in the best pages, I am not writing, but the spirit in me. But my trouble is that I have to be that kind of poet who is in the clear because he has done his public duty. All writers have hang-ups, and mine is To Have Done My Duty.

It is an arduous taskmaster, but at least it saves me from the nonsense of Sartre's poet *engagé*, politically committed. How the devil could a poet, who does the best he can just to get it down as it is whispered to him, decide whether or not to be morally or politically responsible? What if the Muse won't, perverse that she is? What if the Truth won't, unknown that it is?

The most dangerous threat to humane letters at present, however, is none of the things we have been mentioning; it is not the ugliness and commercialism of corporate capitalism, nor the ignorance and alienation of the young, nor the hypocrisy or censorship of power. It is the same dehumanization of modern times that I have been discussing throughout this book: language is reduced to be a technology of social engineering, with a barren conception of science and technology and a collectivist conception of community. This tendency has been reinforced by government grants and academic appointments, and it controls the pedagogy in primary schools.

In this tendency, "communication" is taken to be the transfer of information from one brain to another, and all the rest, the "expression," is noise or meaningless emotion. Linguists construct grammars of basic vocabularies of "factual" words, connected by Russell's logic of relations, to provide a pidgin for transferring information, or to allow for computer translation. These are useful purposes, but they are not what language, or English, is. In my opinion, speaking is an action and passion of speaking animals, directly affected by their speech encounter; the style of speaking is how the speaker *has* his information and is *with* the others, so it is intrinsic to the meaning. In most conversation, the noninformational part is by far the greater; a grammar of English should be drawn from common speech and literature, the heightened speech that has proved interesting—I doubt that there is a general basic vocabulary. What is "fact" depends on how one is in the kind of world one has.

For a long time, say, from Francis Bacon to Neurath and Carnap, scientists resisted using the "unified language of science" that was periodically invented for them. It did not seem to fit the way each branch went about its enterprise; and science as a whole was an indefinite number of wandering dialogues with the unknown carried on by brotherly cooperative (and competitive) researchers. But now science is taken to be a central office in which new data are filed, new theory is processed, and new projects are launched; and the convenience of calculating machines seems to be leading to the rapid adoption of a single language and method. To my lay understanding, this implies —doesn't it?—a likelihood of misinterpreting what cannot be easily said in the one language, and disregarding what cannot be coped with by the one method. Perhaps this danger does not exist in the physical sciences—at least there continue to be important successes. But in the social sciences, the procedure of collecting and processing data and planning strategies has usually proved to be otiose or harmful, avoiding problems or creating worse ones. Evidently the essence has been left out, the language and method are not adequate. Similarly, the use of technology is proving to be disastrous. Technology is a branch of moral philosophy, but the language that is used is not the language of moral philosophy, which is literature.

It is the sign of an ignorant man, said Aristotle, to be more precise than the subject allows. There is more communication in a poem of Keats than in a scientific report, said Norbert Wiener, for the poem alters the code, whereas the report merely repeats it and increases the noise.

Society is increasingly taken to be a kind of machine directed by a central will, and in this structure the teaching of English is turned into social engineering. The purpose of learning to read is no longer political freedom, clarification, appreciation, and community, but "functional literacy," the ability to follow directions and be employable. The question whether a child can and will learn to read with such a purpose is not asked. At the level of freshman English, the manuals aim to impart units of language skill necessary for succeeding in various social roles. At the graduate level, the departments instill the style and format acceptable for work in the "discipline."

Thus, speech is reduced to a code to transfer information for narrow purposes. Conversely, the expressive part of speech, emptied of meaning and of any relation to telling the truth, is reduced to ornament or entertainment, as in the rhetorics of the Roman Empire. Or much worse, it is something to manipulate politically to create thoughtless collective solidarity, like the Newspeak of George Orwell's *1984*.

I do not think this situation is the result of a conspiracy, although those who profit by the tide go along with the tide and have a vested interest in it. And it is not especially American, although our country is the oldest in modern times and is therefore the most mature in this way too. But this disease of speech seems to be endemic to modern times and has appeared in every advanced country, no matter what its economic system or political ideology. Mankind does not know, does not yet know, how to manage the exploding scientific technology and the collectivism which are the conditions of the foreseeable future. I say does not "yet" know because we are an inventive species. But unfortunately we come across only when we are in trouble, and we may again have to go through something like the Thirty Years' War.

Since I started by mentioning the humanists, let me come on at the end like Erasmus (perhaps it is his tricentennial—his birthday was in 1469?). Just now the method of literature is indispensable: to find and say the humanism in new science, the morality in technology, and the community and individuality in collectivism.

PART THREE

Legitimacy

Chapter 9

i

During the thirties, dissident young people received a thorough incidental education in political economy. In the reality of the unemployment and foreclosures of the Depression, the militant labor movement, and the economic strategies of the New Deal, the in-fighting of Left sects added up to a remarkably subtle analysis of the "System" of production and distribution. Marxian, Keynesian, managerial, technocratic, and fascist theories provided adequate terms for discussion.

American students today are provokingly uninterested in economics, even—or especially—when they talk socialism. (Polish or Czechoslovak youth are more interested.) This is probably because in affluent countries the classic economic problems of scarcity of goods and exploitation of labor have diminished in importance. The business cycle and the falling rate of profit seem to have been tamed. Many are poor and many are outcast, but the causes are seen as political and moral. The "System" that the young oppose has to do with Power, status, credentials, alienation, and social engineering; the fussy economic details, such as inflation, hidden costs, artificial demand, monopoly, balance of payments, are surprisingly little mentioned; and no alternative economic model is proposed. The problems that arise from the stage of our technology, e.g. collectivity and automation, also seem to be uninteresting.

In the underdeveloped countries, for the majority of mankind, there *is* increasing scarcity and drudgery, and American radical students are indignant about imperialism and colonialism. But here again, the older economic analysis of imperialism, in terms of raw materials and native labor, is not very relevant for us. The total foreign trade of the United States is a small fraction of the Gross National Product, and the tiny colonial portion could vanish with most of us not noticing the difference. (To be sure, that "tiny portion" is an enormity for people in Latin America.) Rather, it is politically outrageous for a very few corporations to involve our whole society in dirty wars, and there is enthusiasm for movements of national liberation. And there is something immoral in the United States, with a small fraction of the world's population, disposing of more than half of the world's wealth, even if we do *not* get most of it out of natives' hides. Unfortunately, in their outrage, the young radicals are not much concerned about the fussy details of how to give foreign aid that will do more good than harm, or how to organize One World.

On the other hand, the young of the sixties have had their own real experiences, sitting in and being jailed, demonstrating in vain, resisting the draft, frustrated in the campaign of '68, defying authority in schools and on the streets, and being beaten by the police. These, as I have said, have given them an incidental education in the fundamentals of political science, the premises of allegiance, authority, and legitimacy by which political societies operate at all. And the present in-fighting of the Left sects has largely had to do with political and sociological problems: Are students a class? Are outcast races a class? How to build a movement? Can one get power without centralized discipline? Do we want "power" or to be let alone? Is civil disobedience political or merely moral? Is a hippie political?

But the theoretical framework for discussion has been meager. Learning by doing, the young have rediscovered a kind of populism, "participatory democracy"; they have been seduced by theories of mountain guerrilla warfare and putschism; and some of them like to quote Chairman Mao that political power comes from the barrel of a gun. In my opinion, they have done some good thinking about community development. Yet I have heard little analysis of sovereignty and law, authority and legitimacy, in modern industrial and urban conditions, though it is about these that there is now evidently a profound conflict. The crisis of legitimacy is deeper than political revolution; it is what I have here been calling religious: the young have ceased to "believe" in something, and the disbelief occurs at progressively earlier years. Finally what is at stake is not the legitimacy of American authority but of any authority.

In the vacuum of historical knowledge and philosophical criticism, young protesters are too ready to concede (or boast) that they are lawless and civilly disobedient. And the powers that be—police, school administrators, mayors, and editorial writers—are able to sound off and practice clichés about Law and Order that are certainly not American political science. So it is useful to make academic remarks about some elementary topics. Also, as an older protester in an ambiguous legal climate, maybe it is wise to rehearse my case. (I am editing this in September 1969. The conviction of Dr. Spock for conspiring to resist the draft has been reversed; two other conspirators are to be retried; and seven other co-conspirators (including myself) are in the peculiar limbo that the Attorney General has put us: though he has called us felons, he has not yet chosen to indict us.)

i i

Authorities talk about Law and Order and Due Process as if these things had an absolute sanction: Without them there can be no negotiation, whether the situation is a riot, a strike of municipal employees, a student protest against the manufacturer of napalm, a black man disrupting a church service, young men burning draft cards. The tone is curiously theocratic, as if the Law existed by divine right. The practice is all the more irksome when, in complex governments and bureaucracies, the due process of law is very much determined by administrators; and almost any behavior during an incident can be and has been called resisting arrest. "The powers that be are ordained by God."

It is a difficult question why the public stands for this, and I shall try to answer it later. Law and Order sounds like a fantasy of the authoritarian personality, in whom the "Sovereign" has been internalized from childhood and has a nonrational charisma; but although this psychology does exist, by and large the Americans are not conformist in this way. Indeed, they have become increasingly skeptical, or cynical, about both their moral code and the justice of the Law, at the same time that they resort more readily to arbitrary or violent suppression of deviation or infringement.

The "reasons" given in editorials are that we must have safe streets, that in a democracy there is a due process for changing the laws, that violation is contagious and we are tending toward "anarchy."

But do safe streets depend on strictly enforcing the law? Most editorials *also* point out that sociologically the means of keeping peace is to diminish tension, and economically and politically to give the disaffected a stake and a say. Certainly the classic Anglo-Saxon idea of policing has been to keep the King's Peace and not to enforce the law. Historically there is little correlation between the magnitude of penalty and the deterrence of crime. And in the history of American cities, of course, peace has often been best kept by bribery, deals under the table, patronage of local bosses, blinking or negligent enforcement. There is nothing like strict enforcement, for instance when the reform-minded *Daily News* makes the police close Eighth Avenue bars to stamp out prostitution, to cause unnecessary suffering. In the complex circumstances of modern life, tardy legislation, and slow adjudication, the extralegal is often more likely to give rough justice. And at least in the case of New York, lenient enforcement—"it is not worthwhile to endanger life to stop looting"—seems as yet (July 1969) to have had less explosive effects than strict enforcement elsewhere.

Even when it is not substantively unjust, Law and Order is a cultural style of those who know the ropes, have access to lawyers, and are not habitually on the verge of animal despair. Such a high style, however convenient for civil society, cannot be taught by tanks and mace. Then it is dismaying that a well-intentioned body like the President's Commission on Civil Disorders regards Order and Due Process as a neutral platform on which to discuss substantive remedies. It fails to see that, to an oppressed group, just these things are the usual intolerable hang-up of White Power: theft, repression, and run-around. Needless to say, I don't know a tidy solution to this dilemma; abridging due process does not guarantee good sense either. But it *can* be a way of making a complaint be taken seriously.

I do not think there is empirical evidence that all violation is contagious. There is certainly, at present, a rash of disrespect and disregard for law, especially among young people white and black, but the deep-going alienation which is prevalent makes it impossible to test a specific hypothesis like contagious violation. The sociological probability ought to be the other way: those who break the law for political reasons, articulate or inarticulate, should be less likely to commit delinquencies or crimes, since there is less anomie; they have a stake and say if only by being able to exert power negatively. Black Muslim and Black Panther rhetoric, and their attempts to discipline their members, point in this direction; and there was some evidence of diminished delinquency during Dr. King's campaigns. A related and ambiguous factor is that a certain number of bright and active poor youth who used to engage in various rackets and hustles, as the only way to advance themselves, now must have gone into political activism as a career.

Jefferson, of course, argued just the opposite of punctilious law. Since laws are bound to be defied, he said, it is better to have as few as possible rather than to try for stricter enforcement. This wisdom certainly applies to the foolish drug laws and other moral legislation, which can only produce violation and contempt.

When a disaffected group indeed has power, nobody takes absolutist enforcement against them seriously. The organized teachers and garbage collectors of New York City simply disregarded the Condon-Wadlin and the Taylor laws against strikes by municipal employees, and they got their way; nor did the Republic fall in ruins. Only the *Times*, not even the governor or the mayor, bothered to mention the contagious threat to Law and Order.

A kind of climax of divine-right theory in American history has been the law making draft-card burning a felony, punishable by five years in prison or $10,000 fine or both. Since burning his draft card does not help a youth to avoid the draft, what is this felony? It is *lèse-majesté,* injury to the sacred sovereignty of Law embodied in a piece of paper. Yet Congress enacted this law almost unanimously.

Certainly, protesters do not *feel* that the law is sacred. If they did, any deliberate infringement—whether by Dr. Spock, a Black Power agitator, a striking garbage collector, or a driver risking a parking ticket—would involve them in a tragic conflict, genre of Corneille: Love versus Duty. Among infringers, I see a good deal of calculation of consequences, and on the part of Dr. Spock, Dr. King, and others, an admirable courage and patriotism; but I have not seen any signs of inner tragic conflict.

i i i

Turn now from this charismatic divine right to the more tonic American conception that the sanction of law is the social compact of the sovereign people. This is the myth according to which we have made ourselves and, I believe, must continue to be. In this conception, in the kinds of cases we are concerned with, it is rarely necessary to speak of "civil disobedience" or "lawlessness." What social promises do people actually consider binding? There prove to be drastic limitations. Let me list half a dozen that are relevant.

(Of course, we cannot rely on the hypothesis of compact, or on any other single explanation, to account for the real force of law. We must include custom, inertia, pre-rational community ties, good-natured mutual regard and accommodation, fear of the policeman's uniform, a residue of infantile awe of the overwhelming, the energy bound up in belonging to any institution whatever, so that its rules and continuance have power. Yet compact is not a mere fiction. Communities have, historically, come to such agreements, and we continue to do so. People sometimes immigrate to have a different system of laws. And negatively, there are times when men ask themselves, "What have I bargained for? Do I want to live with these people in this arrangement?" and they sometimes choose exile.)

Since an underlying purpose of compact is security of life and liberty, compact is broken if the sovereign jails you or threatens your life. You then have a (natural) duty to try to escape. In our society, this maxim of Hobbes is not trivial. A formidable number of persons are in jail, or certified as insane, or in juvenile reformatories; and there is an increasing number of middle-class youths who have been "radicalized" by incarceration. "Radicalized" may mean conversion to some revolutionary movement; but most often it means a temporary return to the state of nature. Similarly, the more brutal the police, the less the allegiance of the citizens. If we ever come to the point of an official massacre, I trust the government will fall.

In large areas of personal and animal life, as in the case of vices harmless to others, high-spirited persons have a definite understanding that law is irrelevant and should be simply disregarded. Almost all "moral" legislation—on gambling, sex, alcohol, drugs, obscenity—is increasingly likely to be nullified by massive nonpublicized, but not secretive, disobedience. It is not that these areas are "private" or trivial, but one does not make a social contract about them. The medievals more realistically declared that they were subject to canon law, not to the king. For better or worse, we do not have courts of conscience, but it is a human disaster for their functions to be taken over by policemen and night magistrates.

The sovereign must not intervene in matters of professional competence—for example, he must not make a law against teaching evolution. Every teacher is duty-bound to defy such action. A physician will not inform against a patient, a lawyer against a client. We have recently had cases where a teacher refused to inform against a student and a journalist against one of his sources, and in my opinion these will become the rule. There is bound to be a case where a scientist publishes government-classified or company-owned research because scientists have an obligation to publish. And hopefully there will be the cases I referred to in the first chapter, of technologists asserting their professional right against authorities.

Speech, religion, and political acts like petition and assembly are beyond the reach of the law. These Bill of Rights guarantees can be interpreted not as a social agreement balanceable against other social agreements but as an assertion that there are areas of anarchy beyond the reach of social compact. (I have argued, in *Like a Conquered Province*, Appendix, that this was the sense of the founders.) An individual cannot make a contract to abridge his conscience or speech, or a community not to assemble and complain, any more than a man can contract himself into slavery.

Similarly, the law cannot command what is immoral or dehumanizing, whether cooperation with the Vietnam war or paying rent where conditions are unlivable. In such cases, it is unnecessary to talk about allegiance to "higher law" or conflict with the judgments of Nuremberg—though this might be legally convenient in court—for a man cannot be held responsible for what degrades him from being a responsible agent altogether. And note that all these classes of cases have nothing to do with the usual question: "Is every individual to decide what laws he will obey?" Rather, it is the social contract itself that is irrelevant or self-contradictory.

In reserving to the "people" all powers not explicitly given to government, the Ninth Amendment bears at least several interpretations. It indicates an indefinitely large area of anarchy, like the *terra incognita* of old maps. In the spirit of Adam Smith's anti-mercantilism, it gives an indefinite area for free enterprisers in the pursuit of happiness —and wealth. And on the contrary, in the spirit of Rousseau, it indicates the possibility of a concerted General Will that can somehow exert power without legal process, or have an over-riding claim in the legal process. Just at present, the Ninth Amendment is being revived in Conservation cases, e.g. against pollution: the People have a right to their environment, which the State's regulatory agencies have failed to protect.

Obviously the compact is broken if the law goes berserk, for example, if the government prepares for nuclear war. Therefore we refused the nuclear-bomb-shelter drills, and it was necessary for the government to give them up.

Finally, in human affairs, the bindingness of promises is always subject to essential change of circumstances. There are due processes, such as referendum or election of new representatives to make new laws, that are supposed to meet this contingency, and they roughly do. But due process is itself part of the social agreement, and in times of crisis it is always a live question whether it is adequate or whether sovereignty reverts closer to the people, so to speak, seeking the General Will by other means. No one would deny that there is a "right of revolution," but the interesting question in political science is whether it is possible to exert this right without violent breakdown of the whole structure. It was certainly the intention of Jefferson, and the sense of American pragmatist philosophy up through James and Dewey, to try to devise institutions that would make permanent nonviolent revolution possible. And in the complex relationships of modern technology, ecology, and urbanism —always verging on the brink of catastrophe and untold human misery—this is a crucial question of contempor political science.

American history has some answers to it. The vague concept that sovereignty resides in the People is usually meaningless, but precisely at critical moments it has reassumed a vague meaning. American political history consists spectacularly of illegal actions that became legal and were belatedly confirmed by the lawmakers, with due process added. Civil rights trespassers, unions defying injunctions, violators of the Nineteenth Amendment, suffragettes and agrarians being violent, the Ku Klux Klan, abolitionists aiding runaway slaves, nullifiers of the tariff, and back to the Boston Tea Party—were these people practicing "civil disobedience" or were they "insurrectionary"? Neither. Rather, in urgent haste they were exercising their sovereignty, practicing direct democracy, disregarding the apparent law and sure of the emerging law. They were quite confident, from their sense of their neighbors and their intuition of the Constitution and traditions, that they represented the General Will, whether they did or not. And by the time many cases went through a long, often deliberately protracted course of appeals, the lawbreakers were no longer guilty, for their acts were no longer crimes. The issue is not whether this populist political process is always wise or not —consider the Ku Klux Klan—but that it is traditional.

Hopefully the current Vietnam protest has been following the same schedule, and there will be amnesty and honor for those who have been "illegally" imprisoned. Likewise, there will soon surely be many instances of "illegal" obstruction to get clean air and water and protection from the automobiles; and the Law will limp after.

To sum up, if we stick to a literal social compact, asking what it is that men specifically mean to promise, the authority of law would be limited indeed. It is often justifiable to break a law as a usurpation of right, and it is always reasonable to test it as unconstitutional or even outdated. Thus, by this analysis, it is almost never necessary, except in cases of individual conscience where one has no sense of representing the General Will, to invoke a fancy concept like "civil disobedience," which concedes the warrant of the but must for extraordinary reasons defy it.

iv

Clearly, law has more authority than this among the Americans. We are not nearly so rational and libertarian. We do not believe in divine right, but most of the time most people do not have the sense that they have made a social agreement either. We have to look for a more realistic theory, more approximate to the gross present facts; and I am afraid that it is something like the following—the emphasis is not on law and Justice, but on law and Order, meaning business as usual.

In any society, there is an immense advantage in having any regular code that everybody abides by without question, even if it is quite unreasonable and occasionally outrageous. This confirms people's expectations and permits them to go about their business and act out their social roles. Except in remarkably political societies like (perhaps) the Greek or medieval democratic city states, where politics was a way of life, people don't want to bother making and enforcing rules. As Morris Cohen used to teach us, inertia is the most important energy of politics. If the code is violated, people would prefer somebody else, the authorities, to maintain order—this is a chief use of government in the social division of labor. Law and Order in this sense does not need moral authority; it is equivalent to saying, "Don't step out of line, don't bother us, we're busy." And anarchy, defined as disorder, is a tyranny of inconvenience that no busy society will put up with; "anarchists" are speedily and forcibly repressed.

Americans have always been very busy. But their present sentiment for Law and Order goes far beyond inertia and need for routine. It is strongly colored by anxiety. For under modern conditions both of business and rule-making, people feel not so much that they don't want to be bothered as that they are powerless: "Nothing can be done, even if we want to." With such an attitude, any threat to order makes everybody tight, for nobody feels that he can cope. The cat might get out of the bag. The act of citizenship becomes not vigilance for justice and liberty but rallying to restore regularity and prevent further irregularity. And objectively, to be sure, the delicate interlocking of technologies and urban social arrangements does make disorder dangerous.

That is, the sanction of Law and Order has become the avoidance of anxiety, both neurotic and real. This explains the tone of absolutism, in the absence of tradition, religion, and moral and ritual imperatives, the things that produced ancient theocracies. Gripped by anxiety, people can commit enormities of injustice and stupidity, just to keep things under control. The archetypal example is the involuntary commitment of the insane who might be quite harmless

to themselves and other people, but who have no right
to make us *feel* uneasy by their behavior. We enact dra-
conian penalties for the use of certain drugs, though our
reasoned opinion is increasingly permissive and everybody
is gobbling up other drugs. Minority groups that do not
or cannot shape up must be squelched and kept out of
sight, though everybody concedes that they have just grievances and that suppression doesn't work anyway. Deterrence strategy and fear of the falling dominoes dominate
foreign policy, although the evidence is that they are
against the national interest. Squeamishness and stubbornness can go so far as gassing a campus, a massacre on the
streets, concentration camps for dissenters, sending half a
million soldiers to Vietnam, using nuclear weapons—
there's no telling.

Conversely, the strategy of those who protest—"civil
disobedients," "rioters," "guerrilla fighters"—ceases to be
justice and reconstruction and becomes simply the prevention of business as usual. Lively young people, distinguished
scholars, talented leaders of the poor spend their time thinking up ways to make trouble. More serious: if the rhetoric
is that the System, the business as usual of the majority, is
an implacable enemy, it will surely occur to some minds at
some times that it is plausible to poison the municipal
water supply, cause a regional power failure, set fire to a
crowded department store, sabotage a train full of nerve
gas. Such an event would produce a smashing reaction.
Good, say the crazies, that will polarize the situation—"if
you are not part of the solution, you are part of the problem" (a slogan of both Students for a Democratic Society
and the government's VISTA volunteers!). Those who
hanker for the reaction might themselves connive at the
event to produce it. But it comes to the same thing.

V

Sober resistance movements, to the Vietnam war and
to racial injustice, have meant to ask the question: Can the

modern society we have described be a political society at all? Perhaps not. In my opinion, even the rising rate of crime is due mainly to anomie, confusion about norms and therefore lack of allegiance, rather than to any increase in criminal persons, though that probably also exists under modern urban conditions. And some mighty disturbed fellows will return from Vietnam.

"Civil disobedience" is a misnomer for our kind of resistance. According to that concept, the law expresses the social sovereignty that we have ourselves conceded, and therefore we logically accept the penalties if we disobey, though we may have to disobey nevertheless. But in the interesting and massive cases, the warrant of the law is *not* conceded and its penalties are not agreed to. Indeed, I doubt that people en masse ever disobey what they agree to be roughly legal and just, even if it violates conscience. The sense of the General Will overrides morality and even common sense. (As an anarchist, I think all government and much law are foolish.)

Gandhi's major campaigns were carried on under the slogan Swaraj, self-rule for the Indians. The British Raj who was disobeyed had no legitimate sovereignty at all. It was a war of national liberation. The reasons for nonviolence, which was what the "civil disobedience" amounted to, were twofold: Materially, Gandhi judged, probably correctly, that nonviolence would be ultimately less destructive of the country and people. (The Vietcong have judged otherwise, probably incorrectly. The radical Buddhists of South Vietnam advocated the Gandhian method to get rid of the Americans.) Spiritually, Gandhi knew that such a means—of disciplined personal confrontation—would elevate people rather than brutalize them and it would ease the transition to the necessary future community with the British.

The campaigns led by Dr. King in the South illustrated the drive against illegitimacy even more clearly. Segregation and denial of civil rights are illegitimate on the face of them; no human being would freely enter into such a degrading contract. Besides, King was able to rely on the contradiction between the dubious laws and a larger unquestionable tradition of Christianity, the Declaration of Independence, and the federal Constitution. Once the blacks made their challenge, the white Southerners could not maintain their inner confusion; force and murder have begun to be the work of isolated individuals; the federal government, though late and gracelessly, has had to confirm the protest. There is now less segregation; there are a few black elected officials; the situation will finally change.

Resisting the draft for the Vietnam war, Dr. Spock and Dr. Coffin declared that they were committing "civil disobedience" and were "willing and ready" to go to jail if convicted. No doubt they have had a theory of what they are doing. Most of the "co-conspirators," however, including myself, have regarded the regime as illegitimate, especially in military and imperial affairs, and we are not "willing" to accept penalties for our actions, though we may have to pay them willy-nilly. And finally the public has gotten the message. As Arthur Goldberg put it, in defending the appeal of Dr. Coffin, "A proof that there is a political movement rather than a conspiracy is that it has political effect; and the draft resistance movement has had political effect." This overstates the case but it has some truth. Although there has as yet been little change in the President's direction of foreign and domestic policy, there has been an enormous change in public alertness to the military expenditures, hidden government, wrong priorities, and so forth; and this revives the possibility of democracy.

Ultimately, if our methods of protest can be effective, their chief importance is that they are positively good in themselves. They characterize the kind of America I want, one with much more direct democracy, decentralized decision-making, a system of checks and balances that works, less streamlined elections. Our system should condone civil disobedience vigilant over authority, crowds on the street, riot when the provocation is grave. I am a Jeffersonian because it seems to me that only a libertarian, populist, and pluralist political structure can make citizens at all in the modern world, but especially in countries like ours that have breathed the air of a democratic tradition.

vi

In advanced countries, each in its own way, most of the major social functions—the economy, technology, education, communications, welfare, warfare, and government—form a centrally organized system directed by an oligarchy. This structure is not essential for most industrialization or most high technology; it is not even especially efficient, certainly not for many functions. But it has come about because of the ubiquitous drives to power, reinvestment, armament, and national aggrandizement.

The effects of contemporary centralization on the sentiment of citizenship have been various. Where the tradition was authoritarian to begin with and the ideology puts a premium on central control—e.g. in Fascist Germany or Communist Russia—citizens have given allegiance to the technologized sovereign not much differently than to older despotisms, though they now have even less leeway for private life, local custom, or religion. In Communist China, where the new ideology is centralizing but the tradition was radically decentralist, there has been turbulence and struggle of allegiances. In the United States, however, where the tradition has been decentralist and the ideology continues to be democratic, in the new dispensation citizenship and allegiance have simply tended to lapse: they are too irrelevant. Since they can no longer effectually make decisions about their destiny, Americans lose the sense of sovereignty altogether and retreat into privatism. Politics becomes just another profession, unusually phony, with its own professional personnel.

Our situation is a peculiar one. Americans do not identify with the ruling oligarchy, which is foreign to our tradition. A major part of it—the military-industrial and the C.I.A. and F.B.I.—even constitute a "hidden government" that does not thrive on public exposure. Politicians carefully coddle the people's sensibilities and respect their freedom, so long as these remain private. And we have hit on the following accommodation: in high matters of state, war, and empire, the oligarchy presents *faits accomplis;* in more local matters, people resent being pushed around. Until 1969, budgets in the billions have not been debated; small sums are always debated. From a small center of decision it has been possible to spend a trillion dollars for arms, employ scores of millions of people, transform the universities, distort the future of science, without public murmur; but where a regional plan might be useful, e.g. for de-pollution or better distribution of population, it fails because of a maze of jurisdictions and private complaints.

Then the actual constitution is what I described above: The social compact is acquiescence to the social machine, and citizenship consists in playing appropriate roles as producers, functionaries, and consumers. The machine is productive; the roles, to such as have them, are rewarding. In the galloping economy, the annual tax bite, which ordinarily strikes home to citizens everywhere, is tolerable. (Only the draft of the young hits home, but this was noticed by few until the young themselves began to protest.)

Human nature being what it is, the Americans have accepted the void of sovereignty by developing a new kind of allegiance, to the rich and high-technological style itself. This provides the norm of correct behavior for workmen, inspires the supermarkets, and is used to recruit soldiers. The only national ceremonials in recent times have been the funerals of political leaders and the moon shots.

A typical and very important class is the new professionals. Being essential to tend the engine and steer, they are high-salaried and prestigious. An expensive system of schooling has been devised to prepare the young for these roles. At the same time, these professionals, and increasingly other professionals, are mere personnel. There is no place for the autonomy, ethics, and guild liberty that used to characterize professionals as people and citizens. *Mutatis mutandis,* the same can be said of the working class. It reminds one of the development of the Roman Empire, when personal rights were extended under the *ius gentium,* but the whole world became one prison.

On the other hand, large groups of the population are allowed to drop out as socially useless. They are then treated as objects of social engineering and are also lost as citizens. This too is like Rome.

In an unpolitical situation like this, it is hard for good observers to distinguish between riot and riotous protest, between a juvenile delinquent, a rebel without a cause, an inarticulate guerrilla, and a protestant for legitimacy. Student protest may be adolescent crisis, alienation, or politics. On a poll, to say "I don't know" might mean one is judicious, a moron, or a cynic about the questions or the options. Conversely, there is evidence that good behavior may be apathy, obsessional neurosis, or a dangerous psychosis about to murder father, mother, and four siblings. According to a recent study, a selection by schoolteachers of well-rounded all-American boys proved to consist largely of pre-psychotics.

With this background, we can understand "civil disobedience" and "lawlessness." What happens politically in a country like the United States when the system steers a disastrous course? There is free speech and assembly and a strong tradition of democracy. It is false that these do not exist, and they have been pretty well protected, with some grim exceptions. But what is wrong is that the traditional structures of remedy have fallen into desuetude or become phony, or are terribly rusty. Critical professionals, bourgeois reformers, organizations of farmers and industrial workers, and political machines of the poor have mainly been co-opted. Then inevitably, protest reappears at a more primitive or inchoate level.

"Civil disobedients" are nostalgic patriots without available political means. The new "lawless" are the oppressed without political means. Instead of having a program or party, protesters try, as Mario Savio said, "to throw themselves on the gears and the levers to stop the machine." Scholars think up ways to stop traffic; professionals form groups simply to nullify a law; citizens mount demonstrations and jump up and down with signs; middle-class women go by trainloads to Washington to badger senators; the physically oppressed burn down their own neighborhoods. These people are not subversive; the category does not apply.

The promising aspect of it is the revival of populism, sovereignty reverting to the people. One can sense it infallibly during the big rallies, the March on Washington in '63 or the peace rallies in New York and at the Pentagon in April and October '67. Except among a few Leninists, the mood is euphoric, the heady feeling of the sovereign people invincible—for a couple of hours. The draft-card burners are proud. The young who invest the Pentagon sing *The Star-Spangled Banner*. The children of Birmingham attacked by dogs look like Christians. Physicians who support Dr. Levy feel Hippocratic, and professors who protest classified research feel academic. On the other hand, the government with the mightiest military power in the history of the world does not alter its course because of so much sweetness and light. The police of the cities are preparing an arsenal of anti-riot weapons. Organized workmen beat up peace picketers. There is a bad scene in Chicago '68 and a worse one in Berkeley '69.

I do not think this conflict is much the result of evil motives—though there are some mighty stupid people around. There are few "pigs" as well as few "subversives," and plenty of patriots on both sides. And I have not heard of any revolutionary institutional changes that would solve the inherent dilemmas. The crisis of legitimacy is a historical one. Even if we survive our present troubles with safety and honor, can anything like the social contract exist again in contemporary managerial and technological conditions? Perhaps "sovereignty" and "law," in any American sense, are outmoded concepts. On the other hand, those who have lived in the myth of social contract will not or cannot (it comes to the same thing) give it up.

Chapter 10

i

Of the political thought of the past century, only anarchism or, better, anarcho-pacifism—the philosophy of institutions without the State and centrally organized violence—has consistently foreseen the big shapes and gross dangers of present advanced societies, their police, bureaucracy, excessive centralization of decision-making, social-engineering, and inevitable militarization. "War is the health of the State," as Randolph Bourne put it. The bourgeois State may well have been merely the instrument of the dominant economic class, as Marx said, but in its further development its gigantic statism has become more important than its exploitation of labor; it and the socialist alternatives have not developed very differently; and all have tended toward fascism, statism pure and simple. In the corporate liberal societies, the Bismarckian welfare state, immensely extended, does less and less well by its poor and outcast. In socialist societies, free communism does not come to be, labor is regimented, and there is also a power elite. In both types, the alarming consequences of big-scale technology and massive urbanization, directed by the State or by baronial corporations in cooperation with the State, make it doubtful that central authority is a workable structure.

It could be said that most of the national states, once they had organized the excessive fragmentation of the later

Middle Ages, outlived their usefulness by the seventeenth century. Their subsequent history has been largely their own aggrandizement; they have impeded rather than helped the advancing functions of civilization. Evidently in our times they cannot be allowed to go on. Perhaps we could be saved by the organization of a still more powerful international supra-nation; but the present powers being what they are, this might require the very war that would do us in. And since present central powers are dangerous and dehumanizing, why trust super-power and international organization? The anarchist alternative is more logical, to try to decentralize and weaken top-down authority in the nation states, and come to internationalism by piecemeal functional arrangements from below, in trade, travel, development, science, communications, health, etc.

Thus, for objective reasons, it is now quite respectable to argue for anarchy, pacifism, or both, whereas even a generation ago such ideas were considered absurd, utopian, or monstrous. Or to say it more accurately, there is again the kind of dilemma that I have been pointing to in this book: it seems that modern economies, technologies, urbanism, communications, and diplomacy demand ever-tighter centralized control, yet this method of organization does not work. Or even worse, to cope with increasingly recurrent emergencies, we need unified information, central power, massive resources, repression, crash programs, hot lines; but just these things produce and heighten the emergencies. There is real confusion here, shared by myself; it is not all the effect of base motives and stupidity.

In any case, hundreds of thousands of young people, perhaps millions, call themselves anarchists—more so in Europe, of course, where there has been a continuing tradition of anarchist thought.* It is hard to know how to assay

* In this country, the first time I saw a black flag at a public demonstration was at the draft-card burning of April 15, 1967, that I mentioned in the last chapter. It was, fittingly, a modest little banner planted low, with a small white Peace trident sewed on one corner. Since then, in imitation of the French episodes in 1968, some black banners have flown with the usual red banners outside "liberated"

this. There are isolated phrases with an anarchist resonance: "Do your thing!" "Participatory democracy," "I scoff at all national flags" (Daniel Cohn-Bendit). These do not get us far, but certain attitudes and actions are more significant. The young are severely uninterested in Great Power politics and deterrence "strategy." They disregard passport regulations and obviously want to do without frontiers. Since they are willing to let the Systems fall apart, they are not moved by appeals to Law and Order. They believe in local power, community development, rural reconstruction, decentralist organization, town-meeting decision-making. They prefer a simpler standard of living and try to free themselves from the complex network of present economic relations. They balk at being IBM cards in the school system. Though their protests generate violence, most tend to nonviolence. But they do not trust the due process of administrators, either, and are quick to resort to direct action and civil disobedience. All this adds up to the community anarchism of Kropotkin, the resistance anarchism of Malatesta, the agitational anarchism of Bakunin, the anarchist progressive education of Ferrer, the guild socialism of William Morris, the personalist politics of Thoreau. Yet in the United States, at least, except for Thoreau (required reading in freshman English), these thinkers are virtually unknown.

The problematic character of youthful anarchism at present comes from the fact that the young are alienated, have no world for them. It was the idea of Bakunin in his younger years that it was especially among the alienated, the dispossessed, the lumpen, the outcasts and criminals, those who have nothing to lose—not even their chains— that the impulse to anarchy would arise. But I think he was wrong: he starts out with anarchy and ends with dictatorship. Among revolutionary political philosophies, anarchism and pacifism alone do not thrive on alienation— unlike, e.g., Leninism or fascism. They require a nature of things to give order, and a trust in other people not to be

---

buildings on campuses, but I doubt that these symbols were as deeply reasoned.

excessively violent; they cannot rely on imposed discipline to give the movement strength, nor on organized power to avert technological and social chaos. Thus, historically, anarchism has been the revolutionary politics of skilled artisans (watchmakers or printers) and of farmers—workers who do not need a boss; of workmen in dangerous occupations (miners and lumbermen) who learn to trust one another; of aristocrats who know the inside story and can economically afford to be idealistic; of artists and explorers who venture into the unknown and are self-reliant. Among professionals, progressive educators and architects have been anarchist.

We would expect many students to be anarchist because of their lack of ties, their commitment to the Republic of Letters and Science, and their camaraderie; and so it was, among many European students of the classical type—just as others were drawn to an elitist fascism. But contemporary students, under the conditions of mass education, are in their schedule very like factory proletariat, and they are not authentically involved in their studies. Yet their camaraderie is strong and in some respects they are like aristocrats en masse. The effects are contradictory. They are daring in direct action and they resist party discipline; they form communities; but they are mesmerized by the charisma of administration and Power; and since they only know going to school, they are not ready to manage much.

i i

In both Europe and America, the confusion of alienated youth shows up in their self-contradictory amalgam of anarchist and Leninist thoughts and tactics, often within the same group and in the same action. In my biased opinion, their frank and clear insight and their spontaneous gut feelings are anarchist. They do not lose the woods for the trees, they feel where the shoe pinches, they have a quick and naïve indignation and nausea, and they want freedom. What they really hate is not their countries, neither repressive communism nor piggish capitalism, but the way

modern times have gone awry, the ubiquitous abuse of technology and administration, and the hypocritical distortion
of great ideals. But their alienation is Leninist, bent on
seizing Power. Having little world for themselves, they
have no patience for growth; inevitably frustrated, they get
quickly angry; they want their turn on top in the Power
structure, which is all they know; they think of using their
youthful solidarity and fun-and-games ingenuity to make
a *Putsch*.

As anarchists they should be internationalist (and
regionalist) and create an international youth movement;
but in the United States, at least, their alienation betrays
them into the stupidity of simply fighting the Cold War in
reverse, "smashing capitalism" and "building socialism."
Of course, this does not ally them with the Soviet Union,
which in obvious ways looks uncomfortably like their own
country and worse; about Russia they tend to say nothing
at all. But they say they are allied with the underdeveloped
socialist countries, China, Cuba, North Korea, North Vietnam, and all anticolonial liberation movements. This is a
generous impulse and it gives them a relevant activity that
they *can* work at, trying to thwart American imperialist intervention. But it is irrelevant to providing models or theory
for their own problems in the United States. I am afraid
that an advantage of the "Third World" is that it is exotic,
as well as starving; one does not need to know the inner
workings. Certainly their (verbal) alliance with it has given
the Leninist militants some dubious bedfellows, Nkrumah,
Nasser, Sukarno, Che Guevara in Bolivia. They seem to
be able to stomach the idolatry of Mao or Kim Il Sung. In
the more actual situation of the Vietnam war protest, where
young militants might have had some influence on American public opinion, I have always found it impossible to
have a serious discussion with them on whether it was to
the advantage of South Vietnamese farmers to have a collective Communist regime, or if they should just get rid
of the Americans and aim at a system of small landowners
and cooperatives, as the radical Buddhists seemed to favor.
To the Leninists it was more satisfactory to chant, "Ho
Ho Ho Chi Minh, the NLF is going to win"; but an-

archists might prefer the Buddhist solution, since, as Marxists scornfully point out, "Anarchism is a peasant ideology"; and pacifists cannot help seeing the usual consequences of war, the same old story for ten thousand years.

Historically, the possibility of an Anarchist revolution —decentralist, anti-police, anti-party, anti-bureaucratic, organized by voluntary association, and putting a premium on grassroots spontaneity—has always been anathema to Marxist Communists and has been ruthlessly suppressed. Marx expelled the Anarchist unions from the International Workingmen's Association. After having used them to consolidate their own minority power, Lenin and Trotsky slaughtered the Anarchists in the Ukraine and at Kronstadt. Stalin murdered them in Catalonia during the Spanish Civil War. Castro has jailed them in Cuba, and Gomulka in Poland. In the Western press, "anarchy" is the term for chaotic riot and aimless defiance of authority; in official Marxist statements, it appears in the stereotype "bourgeois revisionists, infantile leftists, and anarchists." They are bourgeois revisionists because they want civil liberties, a less restricted economy, and a better break for farmers. They are infantile leftists because they want workers' management, less bureaucracy, and less class distinction.

As I have pointed out previously, the American young are not really interested in political economy. Their "socialism" is a symbolic slogan, authentic in expressing disgust at the affluent standard of living and indignation at the existence of so many poor people. Historically, anarchists have been noncommittal or various about socialism, in the sense of collective ownership and management. Corporate capitalism, State capitalism, and State communism have all been unacceptable to anarchists because they trap people and push them around; and there can easily be too much central planning. But pure communism, the pie-in-the-sky future of Marxists, connoting voluntary labor and free appropriation operating by community spirit, is an anarchist ideal. Yet Adam Smith's free enterprise, in its pure form of companies of active owner-managers, competing in a free market without monopoly, is also congenial to Anarchists, and was called anarchic in his own time. There is an anarchist ring to Jefferson's agrarian notion that a man needs enough control of his subsistence, or tenure in his work, to be free of irresistible political pressure. Small community control—kibbutzim, workers' management in factories, producers' and consumers' cooperatives—are congenial to anarchism. Underlying all anarchist thought is a hankering for peasant independence, craft-guild self-management, and the democracy of the village meeting or of medieval Free Cities. It is a question how all this can be achieved in modern technical and urban conditions, but in my opinion we could go a lot further than we think if we set our sights on decency and freedom rather than delusory greatness and suburban affluence.

If young Americans really consulted their economic interests, instead of their power propaganda or their generous sentiments, I think they would opt for the so-called Scandinavian or mixed economy, of big and small capitalism, producers' and consumers' cooperatives, independent farming, and State and municipal socialism, each with a strong influence. To this I would add a sector of pure communism, free appropriation adequate for decent poverty for those who do not want to make money or are too busy with nonpaying pursuits to make money (until society gets around to overwhelming them with the coin of the realm). Such a sector of pure communism would cost about 1 percent of our Gross National Product, and would make our world both more livable and more productive. The advantage of a mixed system of this kind for the young is that it increases the opportunities for each one to find the milieu and style that suit him, whereas both the present American cash nexus and socialism necessarily process them and channel them (Compare *People or Personnel*, Vintage edition, pp. 114–22).

i i i

The confusion of anarchist and Leninist tactics can be poignantly illustrated from many of the recent student disturbances. Let me choose the occupation of the buildings at Columbia University in the spring of '68 because I had family in both the faculty and among the dissenting students, and I was sometimes on campus. Bear in mind, however, that in these cases a just account depends immensely on involvement and its nuances, and I was not that involved. For instance, at Columbia, some of those who occupied some buildings spoke with such glowing eyes of their communion, "finally" transcending alienation, that it would be petty to suggest that *anything* should have been different, even if everything had been wrong. On the other hand, a more skeptical physician might claim that certain emotional hang-ups are more lastingly worked out by psychoanalysis, with less backlash of disappointment. Perhaps. Sometimes.

The two original issues of protest, to purge the university of military research and to give power to the Harlem community in a matter affecting its interests, were justified to any anarchist, socialist, liberal, or fair-minded conservative. There are abuses that are so painful and immediate, or so generally disastrous, that they should simply be put a stop to by any means that is not terribly harmful. The war work speaks for itself (in my opinion). The particular local abuse, building a gymnasium encroaching on a public park, was not—it happens—disadvantageous to the community; but it was one of a continual series of encroachments by the expanding university, some of which were outrageous, and which many citizens, including myself, had often tried to stop in vain. The black students, who took the lead on this issue, had a bona fide interest in their community power and behaved well, with little ideological confusion.

The direct action, nonviolently occupying the buildings, was a classical anarcho-pacifist tactic. It has had two important antecedents in recent history. First, the CIO sit-down in factories during the thirties: This was not a gesture toward seizing power, but a statement of tenure, that workmen had a stake in their jobs, could not be locked out, and would not work under unsatisfactory conditions. Second, the sit-ins to desegregate lunch counters and buses: These were millenarian statements that the world already is as just as it ought to be, and we will not let it be otherwise.

This is Gandhian. The principle involved in both these precedents is not the formal Marxist one of ownership by the collective but the functional anarchist one of the natural right to use by the users. It is not "All power to the Soviets, People, etc.," but "No Power but Function."*

For some of the leaders, however, the issues and tactic bore a different interpretation. "I hate Columbia," said the president of the S.D.S. chapter—he had apparently gone there for three years as a driven slave—so he could hardly claim natural tenure. And in fact the chapter was carrying out a national plan to embarrass many schools during the spring with the slogan "Shut it down!", using any convenient issues that presented themselves in order to attack the System. Since to the alienated, who feel excluded, the System is a monolith and everything that is "in" is "in," and Columbia was certainly part of our military operations, it was justifiable to shut it down. In the formulation of *New Left Notes:* "Since we cannot yet take over the whole society, let us begin by taking Columbia." But I doubt that most of the students who participated wanted to "take over" anything, and I am sure they would have been as restive if ruled by the S.D.S. leadership as by the trustees of Columbia University.

When the faculty slowly came to life and the students' justified demands began to be taken seriously—in the normal course of events, at least as had happened on several other campuses, the students would have gone unpunished or been suspended for forty-five minutes—the leaders suddenly revealed a deeper purpose, to "politicize" the students and "radicalize" the professors by forcing a "confrontation" with the police. If the police had to be called, people would

---

* The Berkeley People's Park referred to in Chapter 4 similarly meant the park of the users and improvers. We recently had a case on West 26th St., in New York, where, after a child was killed by a truck, parents, neighborhood groups, and the parish priest closed off the street, and the city had to accede to their demands. The chief contemporary theorist of this idea has been, of course, Danilo Dolci in Sicily: e.g., a road is needed and there are unemployed men, so they build the road and demand pay.

see the System naked. Therefore the leadership raised the ante of demands and made negotiation impossible. The administration was not big-souled enough to take this whence it came, nor patient enough to sit it out—no doubt it was also under pressure from trustees. The police were called and there was a shambles.

The high Leninist theory of shambles, polarization, and final conflict is that the Party will then take over and establish Law and Order. The justification for it is that the monolithic System is so evil and rotten that its total dissolution is necessary and indeed inevitable. It is interesting to contrast the anarchist idea of inevitable violence, e.g. Malatesta: "We just try to live and do our work, but they interfere with us, so there is a fight." Or Kropotkin, during the October revolution, said that he could not support Lenin but he would not oppose him, since the violent upheaval was like a volcano, an outburst of natural forces suppressed for ages; and he predicted, with colossal miscalculation, that after things calmed down in a year or two the real social revolution, of the populists, in 1905 and February 1917, would proceed on its majestic course. (In fact, the subsequent fifty years have looked very like Czarism at a later stage of industrialization, including foreign policy. It is not an unfair debater's point against Kropotkin to say that presumably this is what the Russian people want.)

The concept of "radicalizing" seems to be exactly the social engineering that the young object to. It is anarchist for people to act on principle, try to do their thing, and learn, the hard way, that the powers that be are brutal and unjust. But it is authoritarian to manipulate people for their own good, and incidentally expend them for the cause by somebody else's strategy.

And is the hypothesis of "radicalizing" true? I don't know. In my experience, professionals, at least, become radicalized when they try to pursue their professions with integrity and courage—their professions are what they know and care about—and they find that many things must be changed. In student disturbances, professors have rarely been radicalized to the program of *New Left Notes*, but they have recalled to mind that, since they undertake to hang around the young and be paid for it, they ought to pay some attention to them.

Ultimately, when four leaders were suspended and students again occupied a building in protest, the tendency toward authority became openly dictatorial. A majority of students voted to leave on their own steam, judging that there was no sense in being beaten up and arrested again. The leadership brushed the vote aside because it did not represent the correct position, and the others—I suppose out of animal loyalty—stayed and were again busted. Let me suggest that it was because of this kind of episode that many students were turned off from S.D.S. during the following year; but of course other factors, including national events, must have been important.

Throughout, the Kirk administration and the authoritarians in S.D.S. seem to have engaged in an almost deliberate conspiracy to escalate their conflict and make the Leninist power theory come true. The administration decided to engage in a contest of wills. It was deaf to just grievances; it did not have to call the police when it did, and it had no legitimate faculty and student consensus to do so; it did not have to suspend the leaders. Far from showing the magnanimity of secure power, it was pigheaded, vindictive, and, worst of all, petty. For instance, during the strike that followed the police invasion, I came up to lecture a "free university" session on the lawn—my topic was the subject of this chapter, Anarchist versus Leninist ideas of revolution—and I found that the sprinklers had been ordered to be kept going all day in order to make everybody as uncomfortable as possible. Another time, I came up to speak at a rally at the Sundial, and a sweeper was instructed to move a noisy vacuum cleaner to the spot to drown the speakers out. William J. Whiteside, the director of buildings and grounds, explained to a *Times* reporter that "these bullhorn congregations lead to an awful lot of litter, so we have to get out there and clean it up." Opposed to youthful fun and games, this is fun and games from a university founded in 1754.

The most horrible fact about alienated youth is that they are the children of their fathers. As individuals, the young can be freakish. When the confrontation begins, there is a family resemblance.

On the other hand, the action initiated by these same S.D.S. leaders did lead to many good results. It changed the rules of the university's expansion into the neighborhood, where we others had failed. It was part of the gradual professional and public awakening to the war work, the ABM, etc. I have mentioned the community spirit in the occupied buildings which, as in front of the Pentagon, seems to have been remarkable—"We just try to live," as Malatesta said, "till they interfere." When, because of the strike, the sessions of the college and some of the graduate schools were terminated for the semester, the students rapidly and efficiently made new arrangements with favorable professors for work to go on. I remember being asked up to Teachers' College to lead a lunch discussion; I don't recall what it was about, but there was a good crowd, including a dozen professors, in a comfortable old-fashioned lounge, with plausible wine and surprisingly good sandwiches; I was told that it was like this every day, to the pleasure and perhaps profit of all. I am sure it was better than the regular curriculum, though—let me hasten to say —TC is superior to most normal schools.

Some of the leaders, we have seen, had no interest in the school for itself, but others amicably split from them and formed a group, Students for a Restructured University, to devote itself to the arts of peace. For a while, until the police came the second time, the atmosphere on the campus was quite pastoral. Faculty and students even talked to one another.

Interestingly, for the anarchist theory I am here propounding, the most profound and generally satisfactory changes in university structure have since been made by the students in architecture. In this school, there is a camaraderie of the drafting room, including coming in independently to work at night. There is far more personal contact between students and professors than in the "disciplines." And (perhaps) in this kind of profession, there is a more authentic professional commitment by the students beforehand, so they *want* the school to be better.

iv

Consider two key terms of New Left rhetoric: "participatory democracy" and "cadres." These concepts are incompatible, yet both are continually used by the same youth.

Participatory democracy was the chief idea in the Port Huron Statement, the founding charter of Students for a Democratic Society. It means a personal and fairly direct say in the decisions that shape our lives, as against top-down direction, distant or virtual representation, social engineering, corporate and political centralization, absentee ownership, brainwashing by mass media. In its connotations, it means no taxation without representation, no draft for another generation's wars, grassroots populism, direct action, town meeting, congregationalism, federalism, Student Power, Black Power, progressive education, soldiers' democracy as against the present military code, guerrilla organization. It comprises the essence of anarchist social order: the voluntary federation of self-managed enterprises.

Participatory democracy is grounded in the following social-psychological hypothesis (which, in my opinion, is true): People who actually perform a function usually best know how it should be done. Those who are engaged know the score. By and large, their free decision will be efficient, inventive, graceful, and forceful. Being active and self-confident, they will cooperate with other groups with a minimum of envy, pointless rivalry, anxiety, irrational violence, or the need to dominate.

And as Jefferson pointed out, only such an organization of society is self-improving; we learn by doing, and the only way to educate cooperative citizens is to give power to people as they are, to initiate and decide. Except in unusual circumstances or emergencies, there is not much need for dictators, deans, prearranged curricula, police, bosses, imposed schedules, conscription, coercive laws. Free people on the job easily agree among themselves on plausible working rules; they listen to expert direction when necessary; they wisely choose *pro tem* leaders. Remove authority and there will be not chaos but self-regulation and natural order.

Radical student activity has in fact followed this line. Opposing the bureaucratic system of welfare, students have devoted themselves to community development, serving not as leaders or experts but as catalysts to bring poor people together to become aware of and solve their own problems. In politics, radical students do not consider it worth the trouble and expense to try to elect distant representatives; it is better to organize local groups to fight for their own interests.

In some of the most important student-protest actions, such as the Free Speech Movement in Berkeley in 1963, there were no "leaders"—except in the TV coverage—or rather there were dozens of *pro tem* leaders; yet FSM moved with considerable efficiency. Even in immense rallies with tens or hundreds of thousands gathering from a thousand miles away, as in New York in April 1967, or at the Pentagon in October 1967, the unvarying rule has been to exclude no groups "on principle," no matter how incompatible their tendencies; and despite dire warnings, each group has done its own thing and the whole has been well enough. When it has been necessary to make immediate arrangements, as in housekeeping the occupied buildings at Columbia or devising new relations with professors, spontaneous democracy has worked beautifully. In the civil rights movement in the South, Martin Luther King used to point out, each locality planned and executed its own campaign, while the national organization just gave what financial or legal help it could.

Turn now to "cadres." In the past few years, this term from the vocabulary of military drill has become overwhelmingly prevalent in New Left rhetoric, as it was among certain Communist sects in the thirties. (My hunch is that it was the Trotskyists who gave it political currency. Trotsky had been the commander of the Red Army.) A cadre, or squad, is the primary administrative or tactical unit by which small groups of human beings are transformed into sociological entities to execute the unitary will of the organization, whether army, party, work force, labor union, agitation and propaganda machine. In (young) Marxian terms, it is the unit of alienation from human personality, and young Marx would certainly have disapproved.

"Cadre" connotes breaking down ordinary human relations and transcending personal motives in order to channel energy for the cause. For agitation, it is the Jesuit method of indoctrinating and training a small band who then go forth and multiply themselves, and much of the analysis and discussion in *New Left Notes* follows this model. The officers, discipline, and tactics of military cadres are determined in headquarters. This is incompatible with guerrilla organization, for guerrilla leaders spring from the countryside; the guerrillas are self-reliant and devise their own tactics; and they are bound by personal friendship to one another and feudal loyalty to the chief—an example would be Makhno in the Ukraine.* As a revolutionary political method, cadre formation means the development of a tightly knit conspiratorial party that will eventually seize the system of institutions and exercise a dictatorship until it can shape the majority to the right doctrine and behavior. Etymologically, "cadre" and "squad" come from (Latin) *quadrus,* a square, with the sense of fitting people into a framework.

In my opinion, these connotations are entirely repugnant to the actual motives and spirit of the young at present, everywhere in the world. The leaders who use this language are living in the past and are suffering from a delusion of grandeur. They inevitably isolate themselves. The young are not conspiratorial but devastatingly open. For instance, when youth of the draft resistance were summoned to a grand jury in New York, it was hard for their Civil Liberties Union lawyer to get them to plead the Fifth Amendment.†

* Reading Che Guevara's Bolivian *Diary,* one has the impression that he came as an outsider and tried to form cadres among the Bolivians; but this seems to be incompatible with "swimming like a fish among the peasants." Sometimes, indeed, he spoke almost with contempt about the Bolivians who didn't know what was good for them.

† But the poor kids were in a trap. Naturally, they would not incriminate one another, but according to the rules they had to agree to answer everything or refuse to say anything, that is, plead the Fifth.

They will get their heads broken at a demonstration, but it has to be according to their personal judgment and not party discipline. They insist on wearing what they want, even if it is bad for Public Relations. It is the devil to have Movement kids in the office, for instance at *Liberation* magazine; they send to the printers what they judge to be right, quite disregarding the decision of the editorial board. The same has happened in the office of RESIST. Their ethics are embarrassingly Kantian, so that prudence and reasonable casuistry are called finking.

I do not think they want "power," but just to be taken into account and to be able to do their thing. They indeed want a revolutionary change, but not by the route of "taking over." So, except for a while on particular occasions, they simply cannot be manipulated to be the shock troops of a Leninist coup. (I have never found that I could teach them anything else, either.) If a large number of young people go along with actions organized by Trotskyites or the Progressive Labor Party or some of the delusions of Students for a Democratic Society, it is because, in their judgment, the resulting disruption does more good than harm. And let me insist again, compared with the arrogance, cold violence, and occasional insanity of our established institutions, the arrogance, hot-headedness, and all-too-human folly of the young are venial sins.

What is my real bother with the neo-Leninist wing of the New Left? It is that the abortive manipulation of lively energy and moral fervor for a political revolution that will not be, and ought not to be, confuses the piecemeal social revolution that is brightly possible. This puts me off—but of course, it is their problem and they have to do it their own way. In my opinion, it is inauthentic to do community development in order to "politicize" people, or to use a good do-it-yourself project as a means of "bringing people

As has been shown continually in the "civil disobedience" cases, the rules of law were not made for noble and generous people. But I was delighted by the ploy of a young Jewish friend. When he was shown a photograph to identify, he sniffed, "Hm, he looks Jewish. Might be Jewish. I can't say a word. It is forbidden to testify against a fellow Jew in a Gentile court."

into the Movement." Good things should be done for their own sake. The amazing courage of sticking to one's convictions in the face of the police is insulted when it is manipulated as a means of "radicalizing." The loyalty to one another of youth is extraordinary, but it can turn to disillusionment if they perceive that they are being had. Many of the best of the young went through this in the thirties, and it was a dismal show. But at least there is no Moscow gold around, though there seems to be plenty of C.I.A. money both at home and abroad.

V

In anarchist theory, the word "revolution" means the process by which the grip of authority is loosed, so that the functions of life can go on freely, without direction or hindrance. The description of a revolutionary period, therefore, consists of many accounts of how localities, factories, tradesmen, schools, and communes go about managing their own affairs, defending themselves against the central System, and making whatever federal arrangements are necessary to weave the fabric of society. Thus an anarchist history of the French Revolution is not much concerned about Paris and the stormy Assembly, but concentrates on what went on in Lyons and how the bakers carried on the production and distribution of bread; how legal documents were burned up; how the militia fought off the invader. From this point of view, western history has had some pretty good anarchist successes; anarchy is not merely utopian dreams and a few bloody failures. Winning civil liberties from the King, from Runnymede to the Jeffersonian Bill of Rights; the escape of the townsmen from feudal lords; the liberation of conscience and congregations since the Reformation; the freeing of trade and enterprise from mercantilism; the abolition of serfdom, chattel slavery, and some bonds of wage slavery; academic freedom, the freedom of science, and the Enlightenment; the freedom of nations from dynasties and of some nations from imperialists; the freeing of children and sexuality: these bread-and-butter topics of Modern

European History are not called anarchist, but of course they are. In every case, the anarchist victory was won by suffering and usually blood; it has somewhat persisted; and it must be vigilantly defended and extended in its particularity. A new political revolution, even if it calls itself liberation, cannot be relied on to care for these ancient things. In fact, we see that some liberators impatiently brush them aside. But this is not so annoying as to hear defenders of the present status quo, with its freedoms, call those who want to extend freedom aimless anarchists.*

In ordinary usage, of course, including liberal and Marxist usage, the word "revolution" has meant not that controls cease to operate and people dance in the streets but the fact that a new regime establishes itself and reorganizes the institutions according to its own ideas and interests. (To anarchists this is precisely the counterrevolution, because there is again a centralizing authority to oppose.) Liberal historians describe the abuses of the tyrant that made the old regime illegitimate and untenable, and how the new regime institutes necessary reforms. Marxists point out the conflict between the dominant and exploited classes, and show how in changed economic and technological conditions the old dominant group is incompetent to maintain its power and ideology, the system of belief that gave it legitimacy; but the new regime establishes institutions to cope with the new conditions, and from these develop a "superstructure" of belief that provides stability and legiti-

* Unless freedoms are extended, they are whittled away, for those in power always have the advantage of organization and resources, while the public becomes fragmented and inert. New technology like wiretapping and new organization like computerized Interpol must be offset by new immunities, public defenders, and so forth. Labor leaders become bureaucrats and are co-opted, and union members do not attend meetings, unless new demands revitalize the movement. Triumphant science becomes new orthodoxy. On the positive side, however, the spirit of freedom is indivisible and quick to revive, so that a good fight on one issue has a tonic effect on all society. In totalitarian countries it is very difficult to control a "thaw," and we have seen in the United States that populist protest is contagious.

macy. Agitational Marxism, Leninism, works to *make* the Old Regime unable to cope, to make it illegitimate and hasten its fall; it is then likely to take power as a minority vanguard party which must educate the exploited class to its own interest. In this stringent activity, any efforts at piecemeal improvement or protecting old freedoms are regarded as mere reformism or tinkering (I myself am usually criticized as tinkering); they are "objectively" counterrevolutionary; and after takeover, there must be a strong administration to prevent reaction, during which period anarchists fare badly.

Roughly, the original impulse of the New Left among the young was toward the anarchist rather than the Marxist concept of revolution, whereas the Marxists and Leninists of the thirties were Old Left. The New Left wanted to diminish authority, establishment, processing. It conceived of itself as a movement rather than a monolithic party, and it did not speak of cadres. It wanted more equality, but not necessarily socialism, though it was sour on official anti-Communism and the Cold War. It did not at all hanker for power, nor even to bring down the present regime, except to stop it from committing intolerable abuses like imperialism, the draft, and Jim Crow. It was not interested in more State intervention, as Left Liberals were. On the contrary, it put a premium on developing "parallel" set-ups of its own and defending them. In general, it favored the concrete, the direct, the spontaneous, the functional, the personally committed.

We have seen how in the past ten years, for various reasons—the frustration of dealing with a vast interlocking system with many defenses in depth; worsening outrages of that system, such as the Vietnam war and the upping of the military budget since John Kennedy's administration; the alienated psychology of the young people themselves; and real dilemmas of modern times, in technology, urbanization, and mass education, which the young, like everybody else, cannot think through—because of these, the vague but rather pure anarchism of the New Left has been mixed with more verbal and activist Leninism, till some militants now call themselves pure Leninists. But I think that the Leninism is superficial, it does not meet the problem, and there will not be such a party; whereas the anarchist impulse is relevant and abiding, but increasingly inarticulate and drowned out.

(In the fall of 1969 there was another amazing example of a surge of anarchist action among the young, and then its trickling away because the young are too alienated to articulate their anarchism and carry it through. This was the Moratorium, the program to try to stop the Vietnam war by withdrawing from ordinary activity, and protesting, for increasing periods every month. *Prima facie* this was the General Strike, including practicing for the General Strike —just as those around the Living Theater tried to set going a General Strike against the nuclear weapons ten years ago. The idea of it is simply that the business of society goes on by the cooperation of the members of society, but we cannot cooperate under intolerable conditions, and when business begins to hurt, there will be a change. Yet, after a great initial success in October, when several million people of all ages across the country took part, by the end of the year it seemed clear that the young organizers had forgotten their original conception. They knew that they could get half a million youth to go thousands of miles to a Be-In, as happened in Washington in November, but they did not believe that they could get a couple of thousand working people, in transportation, manufacturing, business, services, and professions, to quit work for a day or two. It is perplexing. These young people will bravely get their heads beat in and be carted off to jail, and some will maraud down the street and break windows on some notion of being guerrillas; but apparently, to them, the ordinary functions of society cannot be humanly influenced in any way—they are like laws of nature. If they are right—they may be, but I don't think so—there *is* no solution but apocalypse.)

vi

Let me return to the theme of this book: there is a crisis of belief, the times are like 1510.

In all pre-revolutionary periods, the regime becomes illegitimate, loses moral authority, and has to rule by force. What is peculiar about our times is that, because of the complexity of social, technical, and urban organization, perhaps *no* central authority can be legitimate; it is bound to render the citizens powerless and to be dehumanizing. Then it is necessary to stop thinking in terms of power altogether. The Leninist concept of revolution is no longer an option, and anarchist ideas are increasingly relevant. I do not say that they are adequate—I do not know what is adequate; but I am trying to pose the problem correctly. There is no doubt that in their lucid moments the young see it this way. Naturally, their attack on authority is leveled at the abuses of the present regime; but their restiveness about authority as such, calls into question any regime.

It is the same with pacifism, in the sense of the rejection of big organized violence, whether war or civil war. Internationally, it is clear that we can no longer think in these terms, and this has begun to penetrate the skulls of even those in the state departments of the great powers. It is now quite plausible to talk to ordinary people about initiating unilateral steps toward disarmament, e.g. Charles Osgood's scenario for graduated de-tension, counting on reciprocation. Given the atom bombs, the rockets, and chemical and biological weapons, other peoples will in fact insist on reciprocation.

But also in our civil troubles, for all the argument about violent and nonviolent tactics, it is overwhelmingly clear that the vast majority of young people, white and black, have opted against violence in any important sense. During the past ten years, with hundreds of stormy incidents, the notorious deliberate catastrophes have been that a policeman has been shot, a fireman sniped at, a professor's manuscript burned, a group of scared blacks have carried arms on a campus, a fellow on another campus has blown himself up, somebody has discussed burning a department store, perhaps an office of the Selective Service has been blown up, but no person has been hurt. By far the greatest amount of damage has been done by policemen. I do not mean that any of this is excellent; but we must remember that our technology and urbanism are vulnerable to devastation, and many of the rebels are smart students of science and engineering, and others are intrepid adolescents expert at fun and games. Obviously there is something they do not mean to do. I have said that it is likely that students of high schools, or junior high schools, are likely to burn down some schools; but when it happens, not even principals or guidance counselors will be hurt. The rhetoric, however, is that "the racist imperialist System must be smashed by hammer blows." The Young who say this do intend to bring it down—*and* they are pacifists, whatever their language and passions.

In their alarm about student disturbances, well-intentioned liberals point out that our social and technical system is a delicate Swiss watch that can be fatally deranged if due process is not observed. It is a complicated machine, but it is not so delicate as all that. Certainly it is not delicate about some of the justice that it metes out, in policing, in the horrors it sweeps under the rug, in foreign interventions, in the administration of persons. I myself am a pacifist, but I think that our system can bear, and ought to get, a good deal more roughing up than it has. And I do not much distrust that the young, white and black, know where to draw the line. The most brutal and destructive acts will continue to come from those in power. Their effect will not be to "radicalize" the majority; but perhaps to convince people that this whole way of coping, by power, will not do.

Chapter 11

My son Mathew, who was killed in a mountain accident in 1967, age twenty, was an unpolitical person and certainly had no ambition to be a leader, but was rather retiring. His absorbing intellectual interest was in science, in which he had gifts and worked hard; and he wanted to live and let live in a community of like-minded friends, which he succeeded in finding. Nevertheless, from his early years, he was continually engaged in political actions against war and irrational authority; and through force of circumstances he was sometimes a kind of leader. This pattern of unavoidable politics has been common to hundreds and perhaps thousands of brave and thoughtful kids these days, so it is worthwhile to describe it in a typical example. Burton Weiss, a close friend of Matty's at Cornell, has sent me an account of Matty's political activities there, and I will preface some memories of his similar activities before he went to college. (At this writing, July 1969, Burt is under indictment for refusing induction into the armed forces.)

Emotionally, from early childhood, Matty's pacifism was certainly related to his unusual protectiveness of his many animals. I remember him and his mother medicating and sometimes saving sick little turtles, tropical fish, white rats. There was nothing squeamish or sentimental in his attitude. If he needed to feed his lizards, he calmly caught flies, tore their wings off and offered them; but otherwise he would not kill a fly but adroitly catch it and let it out the door. He gave up fishing around age ten and began to rescue the fish and return them to the river. Mostly he liked just to watch the fish and pond life, for hours, in their natural habitat. He had an old six-inch reflector and also watched the stars for hours, and he spent a summer grinding an eight-inch mirror.

More theoretically, he was an ardent conservationist, indignant at the spoliation, opposed to the use of insecticides. I think the focus of his scientific interests was ecology, the community of living things in the appropriate environment. He read widely in the field. And in method he strongly favored—as far as the distinction can be made—naturalistic observation, letting things be, rather than experimenting and imposing hypotheses. These were also his political biases. They are mine too, but I do not think I am projecting them; we argued a lot, but on these points we always seemed to agree.

My first political recollection of him is the time when, in junior high school, he called my attention to commercial corporation advertising being used in his class. (He and his friends were avid readers of *Mad* magazine and were expert at ridiculing the TV commercials.) He collected the evidence and we succeeded, temporarily, in having it expelled. This involved his being called down and rebuked by the principal.

During his first year at Bronx Science High School he wrote a book report on the life of Gandhi, who impressed him deeply. For a reason known only to himself—he never explained it—he took to fasting one day a week, and continued this sporadically later.

He was active in the antibomb protests in 1960 and 1962. He used to take part in the General Strike for Peace, thought up by Julian Beck of the Living Theater. As part of this, people were supposed to leave off work for a day and picket for peace, so Matty took off from school and picketed the Board of Education on Livingston Street in Brooklyn. Naturally he was captured as a truant and I had to go and fetch him out. This was one of the few moments of pure delight I have had in forty years in the peace movement.

He was at the Times Square demonstration against the bomb-testing when the police rode their horses into the crowd, and Julian Beck was badly beaten. Matty was in the line of fire and came home shaken, saying, "This is serious."

As a junior in high school, he refused to take part in shelter drills and he and three friends who would not recant were suspended. But there was considerable editorial support for them in the press and they were reinstated and allowed to stand aside during drills, which were soon discontinued. I remember being impressed during this incident at how the middle-class parents stood by their recalcitrant children, even if they did not agree with them politically. Matty's reasons for nonparticipation were (1) the shelters were unscientific, (2) in its form the drill was an insult to intelligence (they were required to kneel and hold a book over their heads, as if there were shelters!), and (3) the drills predisposed to accepting nuclear war.

When reinstated, he was told by the administration that he had a black mark on his record. I wrote to admissions at Harvard, where I had friends, asking if this was a disadvantage; and when we received the expected reply that it would be judged rather as a sign of critical independence, Matty had the letter copied off and distributed around Bronx Science, which sorely needed the nudge.

By now he was a seasoned protester, and when he was again threatened with punishment for pasting antiwar stickers in the subway station that served the school, he faced down the administration by pointing out that the subway was not in its jurisdiction.

At age fifteen, as an aftermath of these things, he and other high school students formed a citywide association to protest against nuclear war. This came to nothing.

When he applied for admission to Cornell, Professor Milton Konvitz phoned me in alarm that he was likely to be rejected because he had sent a photo of himself with uncombed hair. Matty said, "If they don't want me as I really look, they can keep their lousy school." They admitted him anyway, but sometimes they may have regretted not following their routine impulse. But perhaps I am unjust—Matty loved Cornell and fought it tooth and nail.

At eighteen, he refused to register for the draft. I shall return to this later, but I recall that, the following summer, he distributed antiwar leaflets in front of the Army recruiting station in St. Johnsbury, Vermont, near where we have a summer home. This made me anxious, since of course he had no draft card. But he explained, "I can't live in fear every day. I must act as I ordinarily would." My guess is that he was fond of St. Johnsbury and wanted to redeem it for having a recruiting station.

Burt Weiss writes as follows about Matty at Cornell (my own comments are in brackets):

> Students for Education, SFE, organized themselves in late February, 1965. Matty was in almost from the beginning. He was most active in the Grading Committee, whose only proposal he and I hammered out. The S-U option in it has since come to be offered in much weakened form by most of the Cornell colleges.
>
> [Matty did not go in for "weakened forms" and in fact, insisting on another option in the proposal, he got his professors not to grade him at all or to keep his grades secret from him. Later, to his annoyance, he found his name on the Dean's list and blacked it out with a crayon and complained.]
>
> Astonishingly, Mathew attended all meetings and rallies of SFE and its steering committee. Such an attendance record was unique for him. He had little tolerance for contentious political meetings, especially when the contention was made by those he loved. When he guessed that a meeting was likely to be angry and unfruitful, he usually stayed home. If he went despite his guess, or if the angry mood of a meeting took him by surprise, he left early. Several times, when he stuck it out, he was moved to the point of tears or actually cried. I loved him then very much and respected his ability to mourn. He mourned that people were acting stupidly, timidly, or dishonestly. He mourned the sudden vanishing of community spirit.

Later that spring, Matty took part in the 24-hour vigil in the Arts Quad and in the walkout while Rockefeller was speaking at the centennial celebration. Nobody got in trouble for either of these actions. But then came the Harriman lecture and the resulting fracas widely reported in the press. Before Harriman spoke, he received the enclosed letter written by Matty and Jerry Franz. [The letter complains that official spokesmen evade real questions, and warns that the students will insist on real answers. Harriman's behavior did turn out to be insulting to college-level intelligence and the students sat down around him.]

In May came the sitdown to block the ROTC review in Barton Hall. All (70) participants were prosecuted by the University, but Matty and Jerry walked out of the hearing before the Faculty Committee on Student Conduct. Here, according to the Cornell *Sun,* is what they said: "The members of the group made a definite commitment to stand by each other if there was anything like differential punishment. Tonight they went back on their commitment. The group agreed that it was necessary to have a collective hearing so that past offenses could not be taken into account. Tonight the group agreed to let them take past offenses into account. Therefore we can no longer be associated." They were summarily suspended, but reinstated when they appeared, just the two of them, at the next meeting of the Committee. They were placed on Disciplinary Probation.

[The pattern here, sticking to the commitment against the great majority, was identical with his behavior at Bronx Science, so I suppose it was characteristic of him and to be expected. I doubt that he would ever have admitted a contradiction between personal integrity or friend loyalty and politics. This is usually judged to be bad politics.]

That was an exciting spring. We kept rushing about in no particular direction, although everything we did seemed to be of a piece. Most important things happened at night, leaflet writing, mimeographing, emergency meetings, passionate revelatory dialogue among friends.

During our months in Europe—fall of '65— Matty had little to do with politics.

[He and Burt took the semester off, to hitchhike around Europe, Matty risking the Student-deferment which, of course, he did not have, since he was unregistered. They did not ask for his draft card at the boat.]

One day in Paris—I think it was the International Day of Protest, October 1965—he picketed the American Embassy. He had expected to meet others there. As it turned out, he was all alone, but picketed anyway. In Seville we went to see the American consul to register our protest against the Vietnam war. We did nothing to end the war, but did get a good idea of the sort of person who is appointed to American consulships.

At Cornell in the spring of 1966, Matty and some friends founded the Young Anarchists. The group never did much but it put out some neat broadsides. Nevertheless, as I later learned by accident, the very existence of a group of that name intimidated the administration and extensive files were kept, including glossy blown-up photos of every member.

[It is touching, and significant of something or other, that father, a long-time anarchist, had never heard of these Young Anarchists from son.]

In May a hundred students sat in at President Perkins' office to protest against Cornell's complicity with Selective Service. Matty was one of the first seven to get there and so was able to enter the presidential suite before the campus police locked the doors. The latecomers were kept in the corridor. Only the "inner seven" were prosecuted by the University. The Undergraduate Judiciary Board, composed entirely of students, voted "no action" and made us all proud. The Faculty Committee, however, changed this to "reprimand."

The day after the sit-in, the University Faculty met in special session to discuss the relation between Cornell and Selective Service. As faculty members entered the meeting, they were handed "A Plea Against Military Influence at Cornell," written by Matty and Jerry.

In the last year of his life, Matty was deeply involved with two groups, Young Friends and the Ithaca We Won't Go group. He was committed to the people in these groups and to the fraternal and community spirit among them. This was the only time since SFE that he was so committed.

In the fall Matty helped organize the Five-Day Fast for Peace, explained in the enclosed leaflet that Matty helped to write. The fast was very successful in terms of the number who participated, the interest and sympathy roused on campus and in town, and the amount of money raised for medical aid [for North and South Vietnamese]. For some reason, Matty gradually became the chief PR man for Young Friends. He was rather inept in that position.

[Again, I was surprised to learn of my son's Quaker connections. His mother and I had never been able to interest him in religion at all, even to read the Bible as literature.]

Also that fall, Matty, Tom Bell, and I began talking about starting a local draft resistance group. The group grew slowly and beautifully, just as Tom Bell explained in *New Left Notes* [issue of March 1967]. When Matty returned from inter-session in February, he was excited about the possibility for mass draft-card destruction, and the desirability of starting on April 15 in New York. Everybody was interested, yet nobody seemed moved to action. Finally, Jan Flora and I were startled to realize how soon it would be April 15. We called Matty, rounded up a small meeting, and decided to go ahead. I was going to New York later that night and so I was asked to find out what people there thought. You were the first person I saw. The rest you know."

[I tried to rally help for them by a letter to academics who had signed Vietnam ads in the *Times,* of which Matty distributed six thousand copies. I also had it printed in the *New York Review of Books.* In New York, Grace Paley, Karl Bissinger, and others formed a group, Support in Action, to give what assistance we could. On April 15, about 160 students burned their cards in the Sheep Meadow. Matty, who had no card, held up a sign, "20 Years Unregistered."

[This was, I suppose, the formal beginning of the Resistance movement, which, of course, had other tributaries. How proud Matty would have been on October 16, 1967, had he lived, that so many who were leaders of the fifteen hundred who then turned in their cards had been his fellows in the Sheep Meadow on April 15.]

For Matty, the most painful occurrence in connection with the draft-card destruction was the breakdown of community spirit that it, and the Easter Bridge demonstration, occasioned in Young Friends. SDS was soliciting pledges in the student union. The Proctor was citing those responsible to appear before the Judiciary boards and suspending those who refused to give their names. Matty and others tried to get Young Friends to solicit the same pledges at their own table, in solidarity with fellow war-resisters. At first Young Friends went along, but then began to talk about backing out. At about the same time, Matty saw the official "instructions" for the Easter demonstration at the Peace Bridge, in which Young Friends, including Epi and himself, had planned to participate. This document had nothing to do with love, fellowship, or respect for the individuality and holy spirit in every person, what Matty conceived to be the essence of Quakerism. There were strict rules governing both the demonstration itself and the personal behavior and attire of the participation. Worse, the document advised male participants to bring along their draft cards to show at the border. The whole thing made Matty sick. Yet his feelings seemed to be shared by only a minority of Young Friends. The group was falling apart in front of his eyes . . .

Matty had planned to go to Brazil in the summer as part of a Cornell anthropological project. His main purpose, as he explained at the first meeting, would have been to work politically with Brazilian students and thereby help to foster an international union of radical students.

[This project was abandoned when, at the disclosure of C.I.A. tampering with American students, the Brazilian students had to dis-invite the Cornellians. Matty told me that previous South American trips had been exciting and useful. He worked hard learning Portuguese.

When Brazil was closed off, Matty at once proposed that the entire group should go to Cuba; this would be a reasonable and necessary retaliation against the C.I.A. system and was also worthwhile in itself. Dr. William Rogers, who was the director of the project, has written me as follows: "I won't detail the debate that followed Matty's proposal. It was the age-old struggle of the soul between the single act of moral purity and courage, and the prudential and tactical considerations of effectiveness. We spoke of Jesus' parable of the Pearl of Great Price. Was this act the pearl for which a man will sell all that he has, in order to possess it? Matty, with an eschatological sense akin to the New Testament, seemed to think so. Considerations of the future did not weigh heavily with him. The important thing was to be moral, thoroughly moral, now. How much longer can we wait?" But Matty did not persuade them.]

Early in the spring Matty took part—as who did not?—in the riotous demonstration which defeated the DA when he came on campus to suppress the sale of the literary magazine. [For "obscenity." It was, in my opinion, tame. The suppression was much ado about very little, and was no doubt the cumulative result of other things. This year, 1969, they have been impounding radical dogs who break the dog curfew:

including Matty's old dog, All Right.] Matty's battle-cry was entirely his own: "Fuck you, Thaler," he said to that unfortunate man's face.

Later in the spring he made it his business to operate the printing press in the We Won't Go office. He intended, next year, to spend considerable time there doing routine work.

During June and July of 1967, Matty worked in Ithaca for Professor Joseph Calvo, doing experiments on fruit flies. On August 7, Matty and I and friends of his drove down from Expo in Montreal, where we had attended the Hiroshima Day youth rally. In his sleeping bag Matty had hidden some contraband, a book of short stories bought at the Cuban pavilion as a gift for his teacher in a course on Mexican novels. However, we decided to declare it, in order that the book might be seized and burned and we could complain to Robert Kennedy. The Customs office obligingly acted up in the face of our high literary disdain, so we had fun planning our indignant letter. Next day Matty died on the mountain, but I sent the letter and have followed up with a suit by the Civil Liberties Union.

iii

Matty refused to register for the draft on general pacifist grounds—the subsequent worsening of the Vietnam war confirmed what he already knew.

Without a draft card, he continued his overt antiwar activity and indeed stepped it up, but this was not, I think, in order to force a showdown, but because of Vietnam. I never saw any sign that he courted going to jail. He did not regard himself in any way as a Witness. On the other hand, he was entirely too open to live "underground," whatever that might mean. And the "tactical" approach, of trying for C.O. or accepting a student deferment in order to carry on revolutionary activity, was also against his disposition; he could not live on an ambiguous basis. Besides, he believed it was bad politics. His enthusiasm for the mass draft-card burning meant that he believed in open massive noncooperation and active nonviolent resistance. (Of course, I do not know if he would have changed his mind about this in the past two years, as has his friend Bruce Dancis.) His eyes used to twinkle at the idea of "nonviolent terrorism," e.g. if one is arrested, five others burn their cards on the courthouse steps.

The F.B.I. first got in touch with him in November 1966, purportedly about a classmate applying for C.O., for whom Matty had agreed to be a reference! This was his idea of "acting as he ordinarily would"; these young people do not seem to understand rational casuistry. The F.B.I. visited him as a nonregistrant in March 1967 and set the wheels of prosecution going.

Matty's approach—to "do nothing"—is appropriate, in my opinion, only to young people who are sure of their own integrity and the human use of their own developing careers, and who therefore do not need to appoint themselves or affirm themselves to be resisters against injustice. Matty had this confidence. Besides, he was a balky animal; he would have found it impossibly humiliating, paralyzing, to try to move his feet toward anything he strongly disbelieved in, such as filling out a draft form, or applying for C.O., or even writing a letter of defiance to Selective Service. He was not, in my experience, "rebellious," defiant of authority as such; but he had to recognize the authority. And he had certainly learned that authority was very often irrational, petty, dishonest, and sometimes not benevolent. The school administrators he had dealt with were not models of magnanimity, American democracy, or even simple honor; and these are the only officials that a growing boy is likely to know, unless he is a juvenile delinquent or on relief. Matty was also unusually stubborn in another sense; he had to do things his own way, at his own pace, according to his own slowly developing concern or fantasy. This was often too slow for other people's wishes, including mine, but there was no hurrying him. Once he cared, he acted with energy and determination.

He refused to be a leader; and indeed at Cornell, as at Berkeley in its best days, having leaders was generally regarded as a poor form of social organization. Groups were supposed to grow molecularly. Yet it is clear in the above accounts that he often did lead. But this was because he acted according to his own belief, without ambition or ideology. He was frank, loyal, and consistent, and his integrity was legendary. If, in an action, he was among the first, or seemed to be the most intransigent and unwilling to compromise, it was not that he was brash or doctrinaire but because of some elementary principle, as he saw it. Naturally, then, others found security in him and went along. So far as I can discover, he had no enemies. Even administrators liked him, and sent me touching letters of condolence at his death. His lust for community seems to have been equal to my own, but he had more luck with it.

After he became seriously illegal at eighteen, he, like others in a similar plight, showed signs of anxiety, an occasional tightness, a certain hardness. This roused my indignation more than anything else, that the brute mechanical power of the State was distorting the lives of these excellent youth. For nothing. For far worse than nothing—abstract conformity, empty power, overseas murder. Yet in Matty's case at least, his formula of dismissing fear, and acting as he ordinarily would, seemed to work spectacularly. Once he had made the hard choice, or the natural one—it often comes to the same thing—he threw himself into all his activities with increased enthusiasm, new energy was released, and during this period—whatever the causal relationship—he embarked on an uninterrupted and pretty happy love affair with Epi Epton, who shared his convictions; this of course must have increased his security, assertiveness, and courage.

As I said at the outset, Matty was not essentially political; he was politically active only by duty, on principle. Rather, he was a daring swimmer, a pretty good handball player. He would patiently grind a telescope, test it, go back and do it over. He jeopardized his nonexistent deferment and took off for Europe because he felt like it. He had found a method of meditation that suited him. Hungry for music, he sat for hours at the piano and was in charge of selecting records in the music library. He was an honors student in anthropology and he was—so Professor Calvo and Dr. Elizabeth Keller have told me—beginning to do original work in genetics. But his political activity blessed him with friends and community.

My own hope was that, after he was arrested, he would —having fought as far as it would go—skip bail and go to Canada, since jail did not seem to be a splendid environment, at least for him. He said he would make up his mind about this when necessary. He had looked into it and made connections, so that it would be possible for him to work politically in Canada.

Every pacifist career is individual, a unique balance of forces, including the shared hope that other human beings will become equally autonomous. Most people want peace and freedom, but there are no pacifist or anarchist masses.

As I review my son's brief pacifist career, the following seems to have been his philosophy: He had a will to protect life in all its forms and to conserve the conditions for it. With this, he had a kind of admiring trust in the providence of natural arrangement and liked to gaze at them. He felt that human beings too could form a natural and wise community and he was daringly loyal to this possibility. He was astonished to see people act with timidity, pettiness, or violence. Yet he was by no means naïve. He knew that people in power and people bureaucratized are untrustworthy, and that one has to be prepared for their stupidity and dishonesty and confront them. (I don't know if he thought they were malevolent.) As for himself, he felt that there was plenty of time to brood and mull and observe and wait for the spirit. The spirit did not delay; there was no need for pressuring or forcing things to a vote. What he himself could do to help was to be open to the facts, honest in speech, and as consistent as possible. When a practical idea occurred to him, it was never complicated or dilatory but always a simplification and a way of at once coming across.

Chapter 12

i

They say the cities of America are becoming ungovernable. If we can believe Lord Bryce and Lincoln Steffens, the cities never were governed very legally; they were too heterogeneous in population, untraditional, and planless. But perhaps a combination of corruption, ward and ethnic politics, cynicism, resignation, and indignant movements for reform constituted the kind of rough acceptance that we call legitimacy. Nowadays, paradoxically, when there is more civil service and unquestionably more honesty, there is more breakdown of civil functioning and less civil peace, and those in power try to keep control by illegitimate force.

A chief cause of trouble, of course, is that the cities, too, are caught in the national, and international, trap of militarism, grotesque priorities, inflated costs, and misused technology. But there are two main problems specific to the cities as such: cities are ungovernable because there aren't enough citizens, people who feel the city is theirs and care for it; and the present urban areas are both too extensive and too dense to be technically and fiscally workable, even with wise management.

Because of the lack of citizenship, there are suburban flight and the privatism of the well-to-do; and the vandalism and riot of the poor, especially the young, who have newly immigrated from the South and Spanish America. After a certain extent and density, unworkability shows up as a sudden disproportionate increase in costs for city services and in congestion, pollution, noise, and social complexity that are beyond tolerable levels. These two kinds of cause aggravate each other. The flight of the middle class diminishes the tax base and the number of those who have the levers of influence for reform. The anomie of the poor increases the costs for policing, welfare, remedial schooling, and so forth. Deteriorating environment and rising costs drive away those who have the option to leave, and further alienate and madden those who must stay.

The mayor of New York has said that it would take $50 billion additional, over ten years, to make New York livable. That kind of money will not be available; and if it were spent on the usual liberal remedies, it might do more harm than good.

i i

The right remedy that has been proposed for the lack of citizens is political Jeffersonianism: to "give," or gracefully surrender, power to the people in their neighborhoods to initiate, decide, and execute the affairs that concern them closely. (There is a good recent statement, *Neighborhood Government*, by Milton Kotler of the Institute for Policy Studies. Kotler has been the adviser of ECCO, the black community corporation in Columbus, Ohio.)

There are two kinds of municipal affairs that concern people closely: local functions like policing, housing, schooling, welfare, street services and garbage collection—primarily, the locale in which family life occurs; and the jobs and professions that people work at, and by which they make a living. There are also, of course, close national concerns, like the April 15th taxes and the draft of the young, but it is local life and occupations that make up the city. And in these matters, according to Jeffersonian theory, people know the score and are competent to govern themselves directly, or could soon become so by practice. In any political system, citizenship—legitimacy—springs from liberty, some kind of free identification, and must start from local and occupational liberty. In our system, liberty is further refined, or maybe just further complicated, by including a demand for personal choice as well. We must have free communities of voluntary persons.

The drive to local liberty has become the strongest revolutionary political movement of our times, both in this country and internationally. As I have been pointing out in this book, it is a protest against galloping centralization, oligarchy, military and cultural imperialism, bureaucracy, top-down administration, and mandarinism, all of which are regarded as illegitimate authority. And the slogans of liberty have been community control, decentralization, participatory democracy, national liberation, Black Power, Student Power, neighborhood city halls, "maximum feasible participation." People want to control their own place.

By and large, however, there has been little movement toward liberty of occupation and function, in either theory or practice. The apparent big exception, the demand for Student Power, is unimportant because the students are inauthentic as students. There has been little talk of workers' management, or of the kind of apprenticeship and education of the young that are necessary for this. Professional and guild autonomy and responsibility have been readily sacrificed for narrow economic advantage. Faculties don't want to bother and give up their duties and prerogatives to deans. Producers' and consumers' cooperatives are in eclipse. Few talk about rural reconstruction and rural culture. Around the world there are brave movements of national liberation, but these movements have been unimpressive, in my opinion, in providing alternatives to the centralizing style in economic and industrial planning, in the use of technology, in social-engineering and mandarinism, in regional planning and urbanization. Achieving local freedom does not seem to free the new nations from technical and cultural imperialism.

Perhaps the neglect of job and professional liberty has been inevitable. The movement for self-determination has been led by the colonialized and the alienated—in American cities, by blacks, Spanish Americans, and the young. (In nonurban areas, the groups that have been occupationally hurt, such as small farmers and Appalachian whites, seem to have been simply demoralized by the forces against them; society has left them behind.) And alienation, to repeat, is not a good ground for sciences and professions, crafts and classical arts, political economy; though it can be—when conventional society has become dehumanized and illegiti-mate—a powerful motive for new religion, advance-guard art, and revolutionary movements. In the cities, stripped of economic power, social usefulness, and even civil rights, and living in a culture of poverty or a youth subculture which is very similar, alienated people have no other resources than their local political existence as bodies which they put on the line in protest, demonstration, riot, physical fighting.

On the other hand, professionals, small businessmen, industrial workers, and middle-class citizens, who have other resources to assert because of their necessary social functions, have had enough of a stake of money and status in the affluent System so as not to mobilize for their funda-mental liberties, which they are therefore likely to lose. Movements like Wallace's are a cry of alarm about this; but though they are alert with regard to liberty, they are igno-rant and repressive with regard to the institutional changes that are required. Many of the middle-class young are not co-opted like their professional and businessman fathers, but as we have seen, they make a point of not knowing anything.

Among the young of the poor, alienation shows up most poignantly in the attitude toward "menial jobs." Often, maybe very often, there is nothing menial about the job in the kind of work, the usefulness of the product, the possible interpersonal relations, and even the pay; it is made menial by social imputation—for example, if white youth who used to do the work have now left the field and it is open to blacks, it becomes a menial job. Postman, bus driver, waiter, or mechanic was once considered dignified or manly, and is so; and they will be considered menial, and will become so. A job is called a "dead end" and therefore menial, as if the only reason to work or make a living is to "advance" in status and salary. This is one of the most damning things that can be said about America. Rebellious middle-class youth, however, see their fathers' status and salary as also worthless; they are not interested in the intrinsic nature of that kind of work either, though they would not call it "menial."

The only possible way out of this metaphysical impasse is for the young to do their own productive jobs, as a parallel development, on their own initiative and on their own terms. There has been some functional direct action of this kind, but not much. (The model, as I have said, would be Danilo Dolci.) Nor have attempts at it like the People's Park in Berkeley had a friendly reception. I think that young people think that the "free university" movement is functional direct action, but since the courses have no professional value, the "free university" is not parallel to the official university. In *The Community of Scholars* I described a parallel university, but nobody has taken it up.

Led by the outcast and the young, political action has consisted mainly of physical activism toward getting "power," which has really meant occupying the premises to wrest local liberty. This process is also taken to be the source of political goals: the organization of the demonstration or sit-in provides the structure in which other uses will be discovered. The activist theory, whether of Saul Alinsky, black militants, or young organizers on campuses or in poor neighborhoods, stresses conflict and solidarity rather than program, utility, or final satisfaction. The "issues" are whatever is convenient to rally support and win. Once people control the neighborhood or campus, and the budget for school or welfare, they will find out what to do for their further advantage. Local liberty will produce functional liberty. Is this theory true? I think it is probably true for policing, welfare, parietal rules, improvement of housing, some city services, some small business, and to slow the drain of money out of the neighborhood. At the very least, local liberty is a way of getting rid of intolerable interferences that prevent any functioning at all.

But activism, power, and liberation do not provide a sufficient basis for many other functions. Community control of schools is a good thing politically, but the schooling won't be much better and the children will drop out. Except in extracurricular matters, student power in high schools and colleges is irrelevant. What the young should be attacking are the things that really oppress them, the system of credentials, the unrealistic licensing and hiring, and the draft. Labor-union activism led to important gains but not to a say in the use, design, and method of work, the liberty of workmen as workmen. In such cases, activism does not lead beyond the conceptions of those it is reacting against. Again, problems of traffic, the glut of garbage, pollution, density, renewal, zoning, and the use of urban technology are crucial in making cities livable, but they require a different kind of professional thought and political action than militants go in for or local power tends to have. We cannot finally have good and free cities unless the outcast groups, the professionals, the businessmen, and the organized workers all have more liberty in their own terms and are willing to cooperate. I don't know how to bring this about, but the truculence and disdain of the New Left do not help.

The real obstacles in the way of decentralization and local liberty are not those that are usually mentioned, namely the size of populations, the complexity of society and technology, the necessary economies of scale, the national economy. Free citizens could cope with such difficulties, subdivide administration, simplify where complexity has too many disadvantages, federate where it is worthwhile, control necessary bureaucracies from below. In many of the functions we are here concerned with, there are substantial gains in efficiency and savings in cost just by operating on a smaller scale (I tried to show this in *People or Personnel*).

The real difficulties are political. Central authorities do not want to give up authority. Publics have been so conditioned and hamstrung that they have developed the psychology that nothing can be done in a different way. And now we see that many of the young activists who are spearheading the movement for local power are so alienated that they are not really interested in function, utility, and satisfaction. They are more interested in power, or at least disruption, than in running their own lives in livable neighborhoods. The offspring of black immigrants from rural regions have endured a badly uprooted adolescence;

they do not have many psychological options; their only possible issues are gut issues. But white youths from middle-class suburbs also do not seem to understand that there are such things as stable families, autonomous professions, honest businesses, useful jobs, and civic responsibilities. A good deal of activism for power, liberation, and democracy looks like resentment, one-upping, and a religious striving for meaning in a meaningless world, rather than a struggle for political freedom to function. Perhaps I don't dig.

And I doubt that local liberty is permanently tenable without liberty of jobs and professions. Top management moves people about at will, both executives and retrained workingmen. If the job has no intrinsic value and tenure, but is just for salary and status, its local place cannot compete with better offers. Brains are drained from the community by colleges that prepare for nationally directed professions and technology. Such mobility is fatal for neighborhood government. Suburban localism is entirely specious. On the other hand, if poor people, entrenching themselves politically on their turf, try to restrict themselves to local concerns and, for instance, try to keep their bright young away from the professions and technology of the big world, then such neighborhoods can be bypassed as enclaves, like Indian reservations well or badly funded; but they are not free because they are not important. Culturally, a Black Power enclave is in fact—no matter what is said—in the orbit of American technology, professions, and standard of living; and its liveliest young, after the hectic period of political action, will leave.

i i i

The remedy for the other trouble of our cities, their unworkable size and density, is obviously a certain amount of dispersal; but it is not worth expatiating on this because, unlike neighborhood government, it is not politically alive. There is a little talk of New Towns, but the couple that have been built in the United States are not much different from suburban developments. There is almost no talk of rural reconstruction. These things will become important only when a series of technical catastrophes and fiscal bankruptcies have occurred in the cities, as they will.

The thinking of the public and planners is still overwhelmingly in the opposite direction. Official planning is founded on horrendously increased estimates of metropolitan population in the eighties and nineties. These are extrapolated from recent and continuing trends as if these were laws of nature rather than patently the effect of bad policy—for instance, in the past thirty-five years, because of technological "improvements" profitable to a few corporations but disregarding social costs, 1,100,000 blacks and 800,000 Puerto Ricans came to New York because they could not make a living where they were. (There is plenty of evidence they regret the move.) And this excessive urbanization is worldwide, occurring most in poor countries that desperately cannot afford to lose their rural population and food supply, and are even less able than we to cope with city slums.

In the United States, incidentally, the flight to the city has slowed down—at 5 percent rural population! We shall now see, as has been predicted, that the chain-grocers and their plantations will milk the consumers without fear of reviving competition from small producers. Quality has already sharply deteriorated.

Yet even a very small thrust toward dispersal might have great value for the overburdened cities. In many city functions the difference between intolerable and tolerable crowding is often a matter of only a few percent, for instance in traffic, mass transit, hospital beds, class size, vacant housing, drain on water and power, waiting in line for services. Past a certain point, heavily used facilities become overtaxed and must be replaced or added to with accompanying dislocations. It is these things that make for suddenly disproportionate costs. With many of the gravest problems, therefore, instead of looking for panaceas, we would do better to rely on solutions consisting of 3 percent of this, 6 percent of that, and 2 percent of the other. A small percentage of dispersal could often be a big help.

As a principle of rural reconstruction, I have recommended using the countryside, in its own terms, to help solve urban problems (compare *Like a Conquered Province,* Chapter 4). This can provide a mind-stretching option for poor people whose life in the city gives them no significant options. Many black and Spanish-speaking immigrants may wish they were back home—a thousand Puerto Ricans leave New York every week to try again back home—but the children of these immigrants have no such psychological alternative, just as they have no practical alternative. The majority of slum children grow up to age thirteen without having been half a mile from where they live. But suppose we made it administratively possible for people on city welfare to choose to live in the country and get more for their money, and perhaps added subsistence farming. (This was successfully tried during the New Deal.) Children could choose to spend a year in underpopulated country schools and board with farmers, for less than the cost of urban schooling. The country could provide a better life for many of the lonely aged, and for most of the harmless "insane" who are really just incompetent to cope with the complexity of urban life. We can revive the old-fashioned vacation on the farm, instead of the city-oriented resort. By these and similar means, the city could spend its money to better advantage to itself and its people would have broader horizons. The country would get needed cash and, a more important meaning of cash, rejoin the mainstream of social utility.

Given solid social utility, the esthetic and philosophical motives of rural reconstruction would speak for themselves. There could develop a new rural counterculture, and the land-grant college could become a center of organization for the new rural activities, instead of being a second-rate university. Few would deny that life in the city and suburbs today is pretty crummy, whereas, with modern communications, cars, and power tools, rural life is increasingly good and easy; except that it has become meaningless.

It is pathetic. A young fellow in a beautiful country place is restive. He keeps saying that nothing ever happens there. He obviously also loves it there, but he leaves as soon as he can—sometimes returns. In Harlem, when I mention the idea of a twelve-year-old's going for a year to a country school, I am angrily accused of wanting to "send them back to the sticks"—like their handkerchief-head parents—and scattering their community to weaken their power. As Roy Innis of CORE has put it, "We must find our solution in the urban centers and not go off on little masquerade parties in little newly created rural centers." Obviously he is responding to a few black groups that are planning to go back as a community to the country; for what is the use of having power in a ghetto that is not livable anyway? And then there are energetic and intelligent young white families, post middle class and post hippie, who *have* gone back to the country—it is hard to know how many they are; I have met them in the north country of New England, in northern California, and on the slopes of Mauna Kea—they usually are three or four little families together. They are wonderingly and ineptly growing vegetables. With luck they are guided by some local kid who still knows how, and for whom they provide considerable entertainment. If I recall the Department of Agriculture statistics, it takes only a sixth of an acre to keep a family of four in green stuff for a year if the soil is fertile.

Speaking of England, E. F. Schumacher, one of the "intermediate technology" people whom I referred to in the first chapter, recommends that the government pay people to run small farms, not for any economic reason but just to humanize the landscape.

Classically, a city is the city of its region; it is not an "urban area." City and country use each other precisely because of their differences. In my opinion, New Towns ought to be thought of in this context—often it would come to redeveloping some older moribund provincial town. Otherwise, nonregional New Towns are super-suburbs of a metropolis, and add to its burdens while diminishing its tax base, or they are rather pointless enclaves of isolated new industry. In Scheme II of *Communitas,* my brother and I sketched out just such a symbiotic New Town in its Region; and I must say that thirty years later the model looks more relevant and realistic than when we designed it.

At present, while the cities swell and fester, beautiful

rural regions are depopulating. Instead of being symbiotic, present urbanization is destructive of city and country both. The in-growing urban area becomes socially and physically too complex, and the costs mount. The countryside has been stripped of purpose and people. The city invades the country with city-controlled superhighways, resorts, colleges, supermarkets, and inflationary prices. Instead of profiting by providing useful services in its own style under its own management, the country is further impoverished and colonialized. Instead of encouraging a big sector of diversity, simplicity, self-reliance, and humane beauty, we produce uniformity, complexity, staggering expense, and nervous breakdown.

PART FOUR

Notes of
a Neolithic
Conservative

Notes of a Neolithic Conservative

1. For green grass and clean rivers, children with bright eyes and good color whatever the color, people safe from being pushed around so they can be themselves—for a few things like these, I find I am pretty ready to think away all other political, economic, and technological advantages.

Conservatives at present seem to want to go back to conditions that obtained in the administration of McKinley. But when people are subject to universal social engineering and the biosphere itself is in danger, we need a more neolithic conservatism. So I like maxims such as "The right purpose of elementary schooling is to delay socialization" and "Innovate in order to simplify, otherwise as sparingly as possible."

Liberals want to progress, which means to up the rate of growth by political means. But if the background conditions are tolerable, society will probably progress anyway, for people have energy, desires, curiosity, and ingenuity. We see that all the resources of the State cannot educate a child, improve a neighborhood, give dignity to an oppressed man. Sometimes it can open opportunities for people to do for themselves; but mostly it should stop standing in the way and doing damage and wasting wealth. Political power may come out of the barrel of a gun, but as John L. Lewis said, "You don't dig coal with bayonets."

2. Edmund Burke had a good idea of conservatism, that existing community bonds are destroyed at peril; they are not readily replaced and society becomes superficial and government illegitimate. It takes the rising of a prophet or some other irrational cataclysm to create new community bonds. It is like a love affair or a marriage—unless there is severe moral disagreement or actual physical revulsion, it is wiser to stay with it and blow on the embers, than to be happily not in love or not married at all. The hard decisions, of course, come when people imagine that they are already in love elsewhere; but nations of people are rather cautious about this.

In his American policy, Burke was a good conservative; he was willing to give up everything else to conserve the community bonds. It is just here that phony conservatives become trimmers and tokenists and talk about "virtual representation" or "maximum feasible participation of the poor," really protecting vested interests. A proof that the American Revolution was justified is that the British government did not take Burke's and Pitt's advice. Later, during the French Revolution, Burke was a sentimentalist clinging to the bygone, for after Louis tried to go over to the invaders, there were no community bonds left to conserve.

3. The problem is to allay anxiety, avoid emergency, when dictatorship is inevitable and decent people sometimes commit enormities. There was the real emergency of Hitler, and we have not yet finished with the growth of the military-industrial that was rooted back there. But Woodrow Wilson foresaw the same with the war industries in 1916 and we did get out of it. So long as ancient Rome had vitality, it was able to dismiss its dictatorships. We, however, have trumped up the at least partly paranoiac emergency of the Cold War, now for more than twenty years. We might get out of even that.

But the worst is the metaphysical emergency of Modern Times: feeling powerless in immense social organizations; desperately relying on technological means to solve problems caused by previous technological means; when urban areas are technically and fiscally unworkable, extrapolating and planning for their future growth. Then, "Nothing can be done."

I think it is first of all to escape being trapped that I improvise dumb-bunny alternatives to the way we do things. I can then show that the reasons men are not free are only political and psychological, not metaphysical. Unlike most other "social critics," I am rather scrupulous about not attacking unless I can think up an alternative or two, to avoid arousing metaphysical anxiety. Usually, indeed, I do not have critical feelings unless I first imagine something different and begin to improvise with it. With much of the business of our society, my intuition is to forget it.

4. Coleridge was the most philosophical of the conservatives writing in English: "To have citizens, we must first be sure we have produced men"—or conserved them. The context of this remark, in *The Constitution of the Church and State,* is his critique of the expropriation of the monasteries by Henry VIII. The property was rightly taken away from the Whore of Babylon, to stop the drain of wealth from England to Rome; but Coleridge argues that it should then have been consigned to other moral and cultural institutions, to produce men, rather than thrown into the general economy. He makes the same point vividly in another passage, somewhere in *The Friend.* A Manchester economist had said that an isolated village that took no part in the national trade was of no importance. "What, sir," said Coleridge, "are seven hundred Christian souls of no importance?" The English factory towns destroyed people for the economy. We increasingly do not even need people for the economy.

5. As a man of letters, I am finally most like Coleridge (with a dash of Matthew Arnold when the vulgarity of liberalism gets me by the throat). Maybe what we have in common is our obsessional needs, his drug addiction, and my frustrated homosexuality. These keep us in touch with animal hunger, so we are not overly impressed by progress

and the Gross National Product, nor credentials and status. For addicts and other starving people the world has got to come across in kind. It doesn't.

My homosexual acts have made me a nigger, subject to arbitrary brutality and debased when my out-going impulse is not taken for granted as a right. Nobody (except small children) has a claim to be loved, but there is a way of rejecting someone that accords him his right to exist and be himself and is the next best thing to accepting him. I have rarely enjoyed this treatment.

Stokely Carmichael once told me and Allen Ginsberg that our homosexual need was not like being black because we could always conceal it and pass. That is, he showed to us the same lack of imagination that people show to niggers. Incidentally, this dialogue took place on (British) national TV.

A vital nigger can respond with various kinds of spite, depending on his character. He can be ready to destroy everything, since there is no world to lose. Or he might develop an in-group fanaticism of his own kind. In my case, being a nigger seems to inspire me to want a more elementary humanity, wilder, less structured, more variegated. The thing is to have a National Liberation Front that does not end up in a Nation State, but abolishes the boundaries. This was what Gandhi and Buber wanted, but they were shelved.

Usually we ought to diminish social anxiety, but to break down arbitrary boundaries we have to risk heightening social anxiety. Some boundaries, of course, are just the limits of our interests and people beyond them are indifferent or exotic. But as soon as we begin to notice a boundary *between* us and others, we project our own unacceptable traits on those across the boundary, and they are foreigners, heretics, untouchables, persons exploited as things. By their very existence, they threaten or tempt us, and we must squelch them, patronize them, or with missionary zeal make them shape up.

The excluded or repressed are always right in their rebellion, for they stand for our future wholeness. And their demands must always seem wrongheaded, their style uncalled for, and their actions a violation of due process. But as in any psychotherapy, the problem is to tolerate anxiety and stay with it, rather than to panic and be in an emergency.

Curiously, the half-baked and noisy writing of the young is hopeful in this respect just because it is so dreadful. It is embarrassed or brazen rather than panicky. It is a kind of folk art of urban confusion, and where there is a folk art there might get to be a high art. It is not advance-guard, for they don't know enough to have an edge to leap from. It is not even eclectic but a farrago of misunderstood styles. But it *is* without some previous boundaries. There is something in its tribalism, as they call it. It is somewhat a folk international. And it is boring, like all folk art; a little bit goes a long way.

6. Lord Acton, who understood conservatism, praises the character—George Washington was a good example—that is conservative in disposition but resolute in the disruptive action that has to be performed. A good surgeon minimizes postoperative shock and at once resumes as a physician, saying, "Nature heals, not the doctor." The advantage of a conservative, even back-tracking, disposition in a successful revolutionary is to diminish the danger of takeover by new bosses who invariably are rife with plans. After the American Revolution, the conservative disposition of the chief leaders blessed us with those twenty-five years of quasi-anarchy in national affairs, during which we learned whatever has made the American experiment worthwhile. "It's a free country, you can't make me"— every immigrant child learned to say it for over a century. The same would have occurred in the French Revolution if they had enjoyed our geographic isolation from invasion; the first French revolutionary leaders were the reverse of Jacobin. Danton wanted to go back to his wine and girls. But a defect of Leninist revolutions is that, from the beginning, they are made by Leninists. They have ideas.

7. I myself have a conservative, maybe timid, disposition; yet I trust, as I have said, that the present regime in

America will get a lot more roughing up than it has, from the young who resent being processed; from the blacks who have been left out; from housewives and others who buy real goods with hard money at inflationary prices hiked by expense accounts and government subsidies; from professionals demanding their autonomy, rather than being treated as personnel of the front office; not to speak of every live person in jeopardy because of the bombs and CBW. Our system can stand, and profit by, plenty of interruption of business as usual. It is not such a delicate Swiss watch as all that. The danger is not in the loosening of the machine, but in its tightening up by panic repression.

It is true that because of massive urbanization and interlocking technologies, advanced countries are vulnerable to catastrophic disruption, and this creates a perceptible anxiety. But there is far more likelihood of breakdown from the respectable ambitions of Eastern Airlines and Consolidated Edison than from the sabotage of revolutionaries. Nevertheless, I think the revolutionary rhetoric should be nonviolent, as by and large the actions have been, though there are bound to be fringes of violence.

8. In a modern massive complex society, it is said, any rapid global "revolutionary" or "utopian" change can be incalculably destructive. I agree; but I wish people would remember that we have continually introduced big rapid changes that have in fact produced incalculable shock. Consider, in the past generation, the TV, mass higher schooling, the complex of cars, roads, and suburbanization, mass air travel, the complex of plantations, chain grocers, and forced urbanization; not to speak of the meteoric rise of the military industries and the Vietnam war and the draft. In all these, there has been a big factor of willful decision; these they have not been natural processes or inevitable catastrophes. And we have not begun to compound with the problems caused by those utopian changes. Rather, in what seems an amazingly brief time, we have come to a political, cultural, and religious crisis that must be called prerevolutionary, and all because of a few willful fools.

9. There is also authentic confusion, however. World-wide, we are going through a rapidly stepped-up collectivization which is, in my opinion, inevitable. I have just been watching the first lunar landing, and the impression of collectivity is overwhelming. We do not know how to cope with the dilemmas of it. The only prudent course is to try piecemeal to defend and extend the areas of liberty, locally, on the job, in the mores. Any violent collective change would be certainly totalitarian, whatever the ideology.

Needless to say, I myself hanker after and push global institutional changes: drastic cutback of the military industries, of the school system, and of the penal system; giving the city streets back to the children by banning the cars, and the cities back to the citizens by neighborhood government; vigorous nourishment of decentralized mass communications and rural reconstruction; guaranteed income and a sector of free appropriation. I look for the kind of apprentice system that would produce workers' management, and the kind of guild association that would affirm authentic professionalism. The effects of these changes are also incalculable; it is hard to think through the consequences in our society that would flow from any and all of them. But I believe that in the fairly short run they would be stabilizing rather than explosive.

10. In any advanced society there is bound to be a mixture of enterprises run collectively and those run by individuals and small companies; and either kind of management will either try to be busy and growing or conservatively content to satisfy needs. There are always "socialism" and "free enterprise," "production for profit" and "production for use." The interesting political question is what is the right proportion and location of these factors in the particular society at the particular time. Safety from exploitation, safety from tyranny, flexibility of innovation, the possibility of countervailing power, all these political things depend on this balance. But cost efficiency also depends on it: "For any set of technological and social conditions, there is probably a rough optimum proportion of types of enter-

prise, or better, limits of unbalance beyond which the system gives sharply diminishing returns. A [good] mixed system would remain within the efficient range" (*People or Personnel,* Chapter 5).

It is astonishing that nobody wants to explore this subject any more. When I was young, it used to be a respectable liberal ideology called the Scandinavian Way. Now if I say that a mixture is inevitable and desirable, it is dismissed as "common sense," meaning a trivial platitude.

Since I am often on Canadian TV and radio, I tell it to the Canadians. If they would cut the American corporations down to size, it would cost them three or four years of unemployment and austerity, but then, in my opinion, Canada could become the most livable nation in the world, like Denmark but rich in resources and space and heterogeneous population, with its own corporations, free businesses, and cooperatives, a reasonable amount of socialism, a sector of communism or guaranteed income as is suitable to affluent productivity, plenty of farmers, cities not yet too big, plenty of scientists and academics, a decent traditional bureaucracy, a nonaligned foreign policy. A great modern nation not yet too far gone in modern mistakes. There would be a flood of excellent immigrants from the south.

11. In one of his later books, *The Third World War,* C. Wright Mills had a foolish proposition far below his usual strong sense. The concentration of decision-making in our interlocking institutions, he argued, makes possible big changes for the better if the decision-makers can be rightly influenced—he seemed to be thinking of John Kennedy. But it is dubious if any administrator indeed has the kind of power to make an important change of policy; by 1961, the Kennedy people complained that they could not. And even if it would and could make policy, concentrated power can't produce human results anyway; it freezes what it touches. However, there is perhaps a different kind of truth in Mill's idea. The interlocking of institutions, the concentration of decision-making, and mass communications are the things that render people powerless, including

the decision-makers; yet because of these same things, if freedom-loving people, honest professionals, or any other resolute group, indeed fight it out on their own issues, the odds are against them but their action is bound to have resonance and influence. In a reckless sentence in *Growing Up Absurd* I said, "One has the persistent thought that if ten thousand people in all walks of life will stand up on their two feet and talk out and insist, we shall get back our country"—and damned if I don't still think so, with more evidence than I had then.

12. The right style in planning is to eliminate the intermediary, that which is neither use, nor making for use. We ought to cut down commutation, transport, administration, overhead, communications, hanging around waiting. On the other hand, there are very similar functions that we ought to encourage, like travel and trade, brokering, amenity, conversation, and loitering, the things that make up the busy and idle city, celebrated by Jane Jacobs. The difference seems to be that in logistics, systems, and communications, the soul is on ice till the intermediary activity is over with; in traffic, brokering, and conversation, people are thrown with others and something might turn up. It is the difference between urbanism that imperially imposes its pattern on city and country both and the city planning for city squares and shops and contrasting rural life.

It was the genius of American pragmatism, our great contribution to world philosophy, to show that the means define and color the ends, to find value in operations and materials, to dignify workmanship and the workaday, to make consummation less isolated, more in-process-forward, to be growth as well as good. But in recent decades there has occurred an astonishing reversal: the tendency of American philosophy, e.g. analytic logic or cybernetics, has been to drain value from both making and use, from either the working and materials or moral and psychological goods, and to define precisely by the intermediary, logistics, system, and communications, what Max Weber called rationalization. Then the medium is all the message there is. The pragmatists added to value, especially in everyday affairs.

Systems analysis has drained value, except for a few moments of collective achievement. Its planning refines and streamlines the intermediary as if for its own sake; it adds constraints without enriching life. If computation makes no difference to the data or the outcome—"Garbage in, garbage out"—then, to a pragmatist, the computation adds to the garbage. In fact, the computation abstracts from the data what it can handle, and constrains the result to what it can answer. Certainly, cybernetics could be enriching, as psychiatry or as ecology, but it has not yet been so—an exception has been the work of Bateson.

It is interesting to notice the change in the style of scientific explanation. At the turn of the century they spoke of development, struggle, coping, the logic of inquiry. Now they emphasize code, homeostasis, feedback, the logic of structure.

13. A decade ago it was claimed that there was an end to ideology, for the problems of modern society have to be coped with pragmatically, functionally, piecemeal. This seems to have been a poor prediction, considering the deafening revival of Marxist-Leninist rhetoric and Law and Order rhetoric. Yet it was true, but not in the sense in which it was offered. The ideological rhetoric is pretty irrelevant; but the pragmatic, functional, and piecemeal approach has not, as was expected, consigned our problems to the province of experts, administrators and engineers, but has thrown them to the dissenters. Relevant new thought has not been administrative and technological, but existentialist, ethical, and tactical. Administrators and planners write books about the universities and cities, extrapolating from the trends— and asking for funds; but history does not hasten to go in their direction.

Rather, pragmatism has come to be interpreted to include the character of the agents as part of the problem to be solved; it is psychoanalytic; there is stress on engagement. (Incidentally, it is good Jamesian pragmatism.) Functionalism has come to mean criticizing the program and the function itself, asking who wants to do it and why, and is it humanly worth doing. Piecemeal issues have gotten entangled with the political action of the people affected by them. Instead of becoming more administrative as expected, affairs are becoming more political. The premises of expertise and planning are called into question. The credentials of the board of trustees are scrutinized. Professionalism is a dirty word. Terms like "commitment," "dialogue," "confrontation," "community," "do your thing" are indeed anti-ideological—and sometimes they do not connote much other thought either; but they are surely not what *The End of Ideology* had in mind. And it turns out that they are relevant to the conditions of complex modern societies.

14. An advantage I have had over many others—I don't know whether by luck or by character—is that I have never had to do, nor forced myself to do, what was utterly alien to me. I was good at schoolwork and liked it. From age fifteen I never had a job that was altogether useless, or harmful, or mere busywork, or that did not use some of my powers, so that I could try to do a good job in my own style. This does not mean that I did what I wanted. Sometimes the work was unpleasant or boring and it was almost never what I should have been used for. I was poor, without connections, bisexual, and socially inept, so that I was always driven by need and had to take what turned up, without choices. But I could not do—I did not consider as a possibility—anything that I could not somewhat identify with. If somebody had offered me a stupid job at good pay, I could hardly have refused, but this never happened. I always worked hard in a way that made sense to myself—and sometimes got fired.

It is devastating that this is not the common condition. If people go through motions that do not make sense to them and do not have their allegiance, just for wages or other extrinsic rewards, there is an end to common sense and self-respect. Character is made by the behaviors we initiate; if we initiate what we do not mean, we get sick. And as we see, the accumulation of such motions that are not continually checked up as meant can produce calamities.

15. The time I spend on politics—it is not much time but it is more than I have—is a fair example of how I work

at what is mine but is onerous and boring. As a conservative anarchist, I believe that to seek for Power is otiose, yet I want to derange as little as possible the powers that be; I am eager to sign off as soon as conditions are tolerable, so people can go back to the things that matter, their professions, sports, and friendships. Naturally, politics should not be for me. In principle I agree with the hippies. They become political when they are indignant, as at the war or racist laws, and they also have to work at power and politics in order to protect their own business and community, e.g. against police harassment; but otherwise they rightly judge that radicals are in a bag.

But I am political because of an idiotic concept of myself as a man of letters: I am that kind of writer who must first have done his duty as a citizen, father, and so forth. Inevitably, my disastrous model is John Milton—and it's a poor state to be waiting to go blind in order to be free to write a big poem. But at least thereby, I write with a good conscience. I do not have to be a political poet.

16. In normal fiscal conditions, the way for free citizens to check the government has been to grant or refuse taxes, usually through the parliament, but if both the parliament and the government are illegitimate, by individual refusal. At present, some are refusing their federal taxes, or 70 percent of the amount, in protest against the armaments and, of course, the Vietnam war. (They estimate the military budget as about 70 percent of the total.)

I agree with the principle of refusal, yet, except for the surtax and the telephone tax, I pay the taxes because of a moral scruple: in the present fiscal set-up, the kind of money I get is not really pay for my work, is not mine, but belongs to the very System I object to. I have a comfortable income. I well deserve an adequate one and a little more; I worked hard till forty-five years of age, and brought up children, on an income in the lowest tenth of the population; nor have I found that my late-come wealth has changed my thoughts, work, or even much my standard of living. But most of my money is "soft" money, from the military economy and the wasteful superstructure, and I cannot see how I am justified in keeping Caesar's share from dribbling back to him through my hands. For instance, I am paid a large sum to give a lecture—mainly because I am a "name" and they want to make their series prestigious; the lecture series is financed by a Foundation; and you do not need to scratch hard to find military-industrial corporations supporting that Foundation—perhaps as a tax dodge! I give the lecture innocently enough; I am probably not the only one who can give it, but I do my best and say my say. It would not help to refuse the money, or 70 percent of it, since by Parkinson's Law that all the soft money will be spent, the money will certainly be spent.

I wouldn't know how to estimate the pay that I get for hard work in hard money, on which I would feel justified in refusing the tax because it is mine to give or refuse, but it cannot be much of the whole. There is a hypothesis that in our society pay is inversely proportional to effort. The idea, I guess, is that big money accrues from being in the System, and the higher you are in the System, the less you move your ass. But empirically this is not accurate. Top managers and professionals do work hard for long hours for high pay; those on a thirty-six-hour week work much less, for varying pay; farmers, hospital orderlies, dishwashers, and others work very hard for miserable pay; some students work hard and it costs them money. Unemployable people do not work, for inadequate pay. In my individual experience there has been no relation whatever between effort and pay. For twenty years I averaged a few hundred dollars a year for good writing that I now make good royalties on; I work hard for a possibly useful cause and lay out fare and a contribution, or I do the same work at a state college for a handsome honorarium and expenses. My editor takes me to costly lunches on the firm, and the food is poor. Third class on planes is often the most luxurious because if the plane is not full you can remove the seat arms and stretch out.

The lack of correlation between effort and pay must be profoundly confusing and perhaps disgusting to the naïve young. In my opinion, it is unfortunate at present but promising for the future: it creates the moral attitude, "It's only money," and politically, a soft-money affluent society can easily come to include a sector of communism in the form of guaranteed income or free appropriation or both.

The telephone tax, however, was explicitly a war tax and my wife and I don't pay it, getting the spiteful satisfaction that it costs the government a couple of hundred dollars (of the taxpayers', our, money) to collect $1.58. We also have refused the 10 percent surtax, which rose directly out of the Vietnam war. This tax for this war is like the ship tax that Charles I exacted for his Irish War that John Hamden refused. The FBI seems to be breathing down our necks, but if they arrest me I'll bring up that shining precedent— and they'll be sorry that they picked on me. (No, they have attached the money at the bank.)

17. In otherwise friendly reviews and expostulatory fan mail from young people, I read that there are three things wrong with my social thinking: I go in for tinkering. I don't tell how to bring about what I propose. I am a "romantic" and want to go back to the past. Let me consider these criticisms in turn.

My proposed little reforms and improvements are meaningless, it is said, because I do not attack the System itself, usually monopoly capitalism; and I am given the philological information that "radical" means "going to the root," whereas I hack at the branches. To answer this, I have tried to show that in a complex society which is a network rather than a monolith with a head, a piecemeal approach can be effective; it is the safest, least likely to produce ruinous consequences of either repression or "success"; it involves people where they are competent, or could become competent, and so creates citizens, which is better than "politicizing"; it more easily dissolves the metaphysical despair that nothing can be done. And since, in my opinion, the aim of politics is to produce not a good society but a tolerable one, it is best to try to cut abuses down to manageable size; the best solutions are usually not global but a little of this and a little of that.

More important, in the confusing conditions of modern times, so bristling with dilemmas, I don't know what is the root. I have not heard of any formula, e.g., "Socialism," that answers the root questions. If I were a citizen of a Communist country, I should no doubt be getting into (more) trouble by tinkering with "bourgeois" improvements. Since all actual societies are, and have to be, mixtures of socialism, market economy, etc., the problem in any society is to get a more judicious mixture, and this *might* be most attainable by tinkering.

18. A second criticism is that I don't explain how to bring about the nice things I propose. The chief reason for this, of course, is that I don't know how or I would proclaim it. Put it this way: I have been a pacifist for forty years and rather active for thirty years, and . . . But ignorance is rarely an excuse. What my critics really object to is that I accept my not knowing too easily, as if the actuality of change were unimportant, when in fact people are wretched and dying.

As I have explained, I do not have the character for politics. I cannot lead or easily be led, and I am dubious about the ability of parties and government to accomplish any positive good—and which of these is cause, which is effect?—therefore I do not put my mind to questions of manipulation and power, I do not belong to a party, and therefore I have no thoughts. Belief and commitment are necessary in order to have relevant ideas. Nevertheless, somebody has to make sense, and I am often willing to oblige, as a man of letters, as part of the division of labor, so to speak.

I do agree with my critics that there cannot be social thought without political action; and if I violate this rule, I ought to stop. Unless it is high poetry, utopian thinking is boring. "Neutral" sociology is morally repugnant and bad science. An essential part of any sociological inquiry is having a practical effect, otherwise the problem is badly defined: people are being taken as objects rather than human beings, and the inquirer himself is not all there.

For the humanistic problems that I mostly work at, however, the sense of powerlessness, the loss of history, vulgarity, the lack of magnanimity, alienation, the maladaptation of organism and environment—and these are political problems—maybe there are no other "strategies" than literature, dialogue, and trying to be a useful citizen oneself.

19. I am not a "romantic"; what puts my liberal and radical critics off is that I am a conservative, a conservationist. I do use the past; the question is how.

I get a kind of insight (for myself) from the genetic method, from seeing how a habit or institution has developed to its present form; but I really do understand that its positive value and meaning are in its present action, coping with present conditions. Freud, for instance, was in error when he sometimes spoke as if a man had a child inside of him, or a vertebrate had an annelid worm inside. Each specified individual behaves as the whole that it has become; and every stage of life, as Dewey used to insist, has its own problems and ways of coping.

The criticism of the genetic fallacy, however, does not apply to the *negative,* to the *lapses* in the present, which can often be remedied only by taking into account some simplicities of the past. The case is analogous to localizing an organic function, e.g. seeing. As Kurt Goldstein used to point out, we cannot localize seeing in the eye or the brain—it is a function of the whole organism in its environment. But a *failure* of sight may well be localized in the cornea, the optic nerve, etc. We cannot explain speech by the psychosexual history of an infant; it is a person's way of being in the world. But a speech defect, e.g. lisping, may well come from inhibited biting because of imperfect weaning. This is, of course, what Freud knew as a clinician when he was not being metapsychological.

My books are full of one-paragraph or two-page "histories"—of the concept of alienation, the system of welfare, suburbanization, compulsory schooling, the anthropology of neurosis, university administration, citizenly powerlessness, missed revolutions, etc., etc. In every case my purpose is to show that a coerced or inauthentic settling of a conflict has left an unfinished situation to the next generation, and the difficulty becomes more complex in the new conditions. Then it is useful to remember the simpler state before

things went wrong; it is hopelessly archaic as a present response, but it has vitality and may suggest a new program
involving a renewed conflict. This is the therapeutic use of
history. As Ben Nelson has said, the point of history is to
keep old (defeated) causes alive. Of course, this reasoning
presupposes that there is a nature of things, including human nature, whose right development can be violated.
There is.

An inauthentic solution complicates, produces a mon-
ster. An authentic solution neither simplifies nor complicates, but produces a new configuration, a species, adapted
to the on-going situation. There is a human nature, and it
is characteristic of that nature to go on making itself ever
different. This is the humanistic use of history, to remind
of man's various ways of being great. So we have become
mathematical, tragical, political, loyal, romantic, civil-liber-
tarian, universalist, experimental-scientific, collectivist, etc.,
etc.—these too accumulate and become a mighty heavy
burden. There is no laying any of it down.

20. I went down to Dartmouth to lead some seminars
of American Telephone and Telegraph executives who
were being groomed to be vice-presidents. They wanted to
know how to get on with the young people, since they would
have to employ them, or try. (Why do I go? Ah, why do I
go? It's not for money and it's not out of vanity. I go because they ask me. Since I used to gripe bitterly when I was
left out of the world, how can I gracelessly decline when I
am invited in?)

I had three suggestions. First, citing my usual evidence
of the irrelevance of school grades and diplomas, I urged
them to hire black and Puerto-Rican dropouts, who would
learn on the job as well as anybody else, whereas to require
academic credentials would put them at a disadvantage.
Not to my surprise, the executives were agreeable to this
idea. (There were twenty-five of them, no black and no
woman.) It was do-good and no disadvantage to them as
practical administrators. One said that he was already hiring
dropouts and it had worked out very well.

Secondly, I pointed out that dialogue across the generation gap was quite impossible for them, and their present tactics of youth projects and special training would be taken as, and were, co-optation. Yet people who will not talk to one another can get together by working together on a useful job that they both care about, like fixing the car. And draft counseling, I offered, was something that the best of the young cared strongly about; the telephone company could provide valuable and interesting help in this, for instance the retrieval and dissemination of information: and all this was most respectable and American, since every kid should know his rights. Not to my surprise, the executives were not enthusiastic about this proposal. But they saw the point—and had to agree— and would certainly not follow up.

My third idea, however, they did not seem to know what to do with. I told them that Ralph Nader was going around the schools urging the engineering students to come on like professionals, and to stand up to the front desk when asked for unprofessional work. In my opinion, an important move for such integrity would be for the young engineers to organize for defense of the profession, and strike or boycott if necessary: a model was the American Association of University Professors in its heyday, fifty years ago. I urged the executives to encourage such organization; it would make the telephone company a better telephone company, more serviceable to the community; and young people would cease to regard engineers as finks. To my surprise, the prospective vice-presidents of A.T. & T. seemed to be embarrassed. (We were all pleasant people and very friendly.) I take it that *this*—somewhere here—is the issue.

I am pleased to notice how again and again in this book I have returned to the freedoms, duties, and opportunities of earnest professionals. It means that I am thinking from where I breathe.

North Stratford, N.H.
August, 1969

Author

PAUL GOODMAN, a native New Yorker, was born in 1911. After graduating from City College in New York, he received his Ph.D. in humanities from the University of Chicago. Mr. Goodman has taught at the University of Chicago, New York University, Black Mountain College, Sarah Lawrence, and the University of Wisconsin, and has lectured at various universities throughout the country.

Mr. Goodman has written for *Commentary, Politics, Kenyon Review, Resistance, Liberation, Partisan Review,* and other periodicals. His novels include *Parents' Day, The Empire City,* and *Making Do.* He is also the author of *Three Plays: The Young Disciple, Faustina, and Jonah.* He has published two volumes of verse—*Hawkweed* (available in Vintage Books) and *The Lordly Hudson*—and a volume of short stories, *Adam and his Works* (also available in Vintage Books). *Kafka's Prayer* and *The Structure of Literature* are books of literary criticism. Vintage Books has reprinted several of Mr. Goodman's well-known works of social criticism, among them *Growing Up Absurd, Utopian Essays and Practical Proposals, The Community of Scholars* and *Compulsory Mis-education* (both in one volume), *People or Personnel* and *Like a Conquered Province* (also combined in one volume), and *Five Years.*

Paul Goodman is married and lives in New York City and New Hampshire.